Paint
Quick and Easy

Paint
Quick and Easy

Original projects with glass and fabric paint

Zaresa Bosman

METZ PRESS

Dedicated to someone who believes in me – my husband, Henno

Thanks to my father, whose financial support enabled me to produce the material for this book, to my mother, the most talented woman I know, for providing me with creative provisions for the journey of life; to my children, Pierre and Mia, for their patience and love the past year, and finally to Wilsia Metz, my publisher, for her enthusiasm and perfectionism.

METZ PRESS

Published in 1998 by
Metz Press
1 Cameronians Avenue
Welgemoed 7530

Copyright © Zaresa Bosman 1998
Copyright © Metz Press
Copyright photographs and illustrations © Metz Press & Zaresa Bosman

All rights reserved. No part of this publication may be reproduced, stored in a retrieval system, or transmitted, in any form or by any means, electronic, mechanical, photocopying, recording or otherwise, without the prior written permission of the copyright owners.

Editor	Wilsia Metz
Translator	Ethné Clarke
Photographer	David Pickett
Styling	Nanette van Rooyen
Design and typesetting	Alix Korte t/a Design Dynamix
Cover design	Alix Korte t/a Design Dynamix
Templates	Alix Korte t/a Design Dynamix
Line drawings	Darryl Edwardes, Platform Graphics
Repro coordinator	Andrew de Kock
Reproduction	Positive Image, Cape Town
Printing and binding	Tien Wah Press (Pte.) Ltd., Singapore

ISBN 1-875001-35-2

Foreword

Anyone who can handle a brush, can use a little paint to create a pretty and useful article from items normally destined for the rubbish bin. All you need is the ability to look beyond the obvious to find new uses for items such as empty cooldrink bottles and cans, or sheets, pillow slips, curtain linings and table cloths that no longer look fresh and attractive.

Be imaginative and daring, and explore different possibilities. Don't assume that glass paint is meant for glass only, or that fabric paint cannot be used on anything but fabric, or that PVA is restricted to walls. Try out all sorts of other uses, experiment with different combinations and learn from your observations.

We are surrounded by so many things with the potential to stimulate our creativity – but we have to learn to be receptive when we look at them so that we can take in and apply what we see. You really do not have to be artistic to experience the thrill of creating something unique. And this joy is matched only by the heartfelt pleasure of giving your unique 'creation' to someone special, as a special gift.

Every project in this book has clear step-by-step instructions and you can make each article exactly as shown in the full colour photographs. But my greatest wish is that when you tackle these projects, you will be inspired to use the basic ideas and apply them in your own unique way. Then I would have reached the goal I set myself when I started writing this book: that it will inspire the creative person within each one of us.

CONTENTS

Glass paint everywhere

Canned Frame 14
A Parrot for the Fridge 17
Fleur-de-loo 18
Decorative Stickers 20
Egyptian Queen 23
Make-up Tin 24
Butterfly Mobile 27
Romantic Roses 28
Jewellery Showpieces 31
Brilliant Jewellery 32
Foiled and Framed 34
Trendy Trinket Boxes 36
Contained in Colour 38
The Mirror is a Frame 40
Disco Balls 43
Lizard on the Table 44
Flowery Fan 46
Time Capped 48
Fantasy Lamp 51
Colour me Quickly 52
Coasting Along 53
Sunshine on my Table 54
Candles for Africa 56
Candle in a Ball 58
Tall Lamp with Perspex 60

Fabric paint adds new lustre

Couch Lizards 68
Chairs in Pairs 71
Two by Two Place-mats 72
Rugged Frame 74
Shining Example 76
Beach Chair in the Bedroom 79
Bedding in a Roll 80
From Wall to Floor 83
Glowing Bouquet 84
Dream Jar on a Wall 88
Jar-shaped Lamps 91
King of Screens 92
Jacketed Chair 94
Jolly Jokers 97
Say it with Flowers 98
Fruity Blind 101
Multipurpose Mats 102
Sunny Blind 105
Starry Drapes 106
Stellar Window Treatment 108
Fabulous Floors 111
Sprayed Colour 112
Fishy Throw 114
Put your Stamp on it 117
Designer Denim 118
Reversible Waistcoats 121
Stylish Toilet Set 122
Tulips for Spring 125
Spotted Guineafowl 126

Index 128

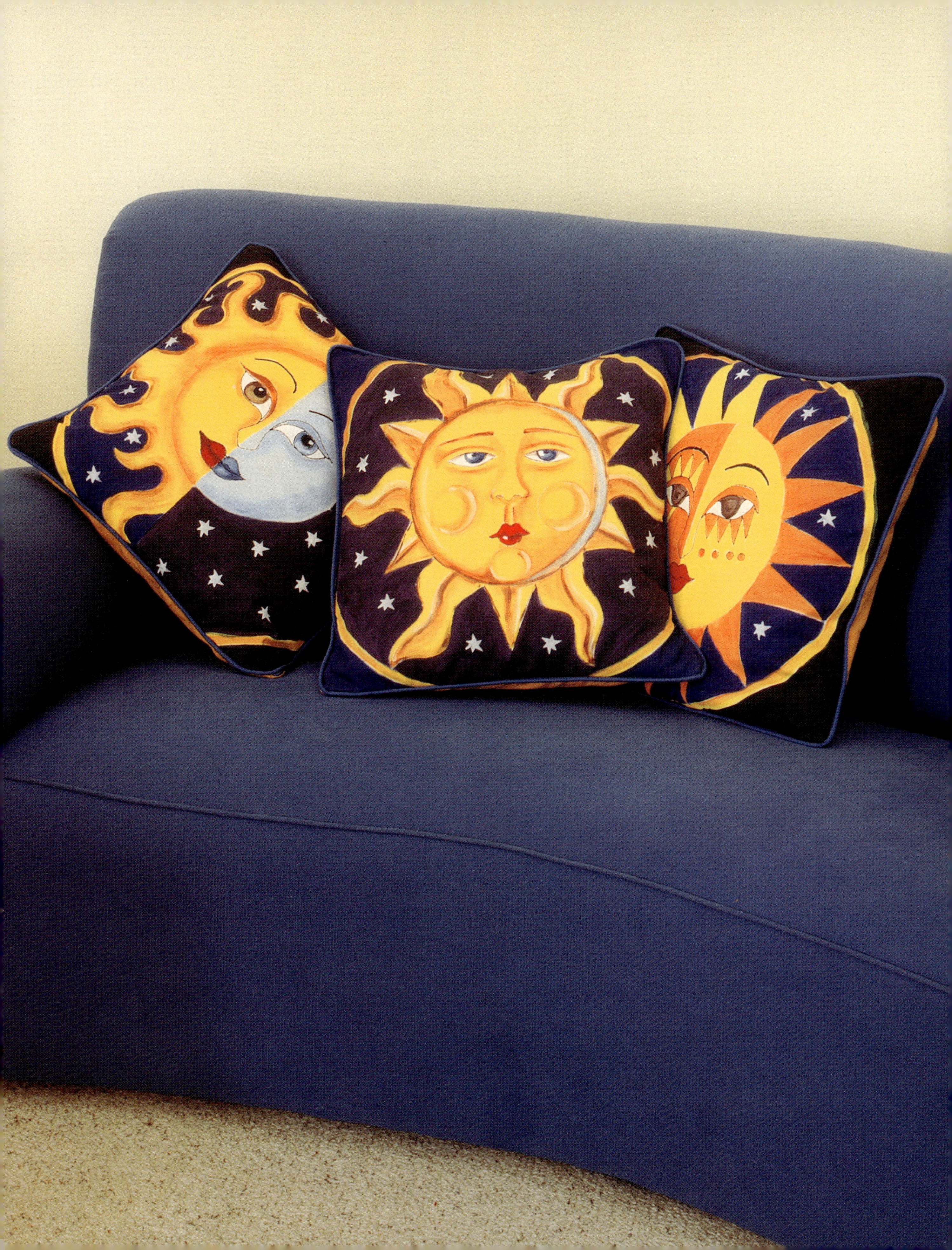

8

PAINT - QUICK
AND EASY

Allow yourself free scope ...

Decorating with glass paint allows you to give free reign to your imagination. The technique is simple and straightforward, and you don't have to limit yourself to glass only. Consider all kinds of surfaces to paint. Recycle junk such as beer cans; and cut, paste and paint them to transform them into colourful picture frames, fridge magnets or unusual jewellery. Or turn an old hubcap into a posh wall clock!

The art of glass painting was developed primarily for giving glass the appearance of stained glass. But because glass is so brittle and has to be cut to the right shape, its practical uses are limited and few people actually specialise in the art of stained glass.

Glass paint everywhere

PAINT – QUICK AND EASY

Glass paint, wooden skewers, fragments of mirror glass, pieces of plastic, acetate, empty cooldrink cans and a pair of sharp scissors are some of the basic materials you need.

About ten years ago I wanted to introduce a group of schoolchildren to stained-glass painting and had to find an alternative to glass. To my delight I discovered something that has never let me down – a plastic cooldrink bottle! I cut out many shapes, decorated them with liquid lead and glass paint and made anything from butterfly earrings to frames for photographs or mirrors, and candleholders.

When I tried to use the cooldrink bottle plastic to make a lampshade, I was disappointed to find that heat from the globe made the plastic curl – until I began to deliberately curl strips of plastic with the heat of a candle flame and the end result happened to resemble a delicate rose-bud. I decorated the plastic rose-bud with glass paint and never looked back. Today I use these crinkly roses to decorate napkin-rings, earrings, hair-clips …

This was only the beginning of my voyage of discovery. From then on I left no transparent or shiny surface untouched! Self-adhesive plastic, parchment, cooldrink cans, perspex, mirrors, tin foil, acetate film and transparencies have all been successfully decorated and transformed into attractive and useful items.

Basic Requirements

Design

Many people seldom attempt handicrafts because they don't have enough self-confidence to draw free-hand. But you don't have to be able to draw if you find inspiration from giftwrap, greeting cards, printed fabrics, or from nature. 'Borrow' patterns and colour combinations to suit the article you intend making. Enlarge or reduce the size of a pattern or design with a photocopier, or use the block technique, and go for it! Place the design or pattern under a transparent surface for tracing (attach lightly if necessary) or use tracing paper to transfer it to an opaque surface.

Liquid lead

Liquid lead outliner is available in various colours, such as black, gold, silver, copper, and pearl. It comes in small tubes and is applied by gently squeezing the liquid lead through the thin nozzle screwed to the opening of the tube. Apply the lead in thin lines to the surface you are decorating. It dries in about 30 minutes. The liquid lead outline prevents the different colours of glass paint from running into each other.

Applying Glass Paint

You can apply glass paint in various ways, or combine techniques, depending on the desired effect:

- A soft brush achieves softer, more subtle shades of colour and the brush strokes are visible. Clean the brush with acetone or thinners between different colour applications. Turpentine is not suitable.

- Pour a small amount of glass paint into a paper plate, crumple a plastic bag and dip it into the paint. Dab the crumpled plastic over the entire surface to achieve a sponging effect.

- Applying the paint with a wooden skewer achieves a rich and more solid colour effect. Dip the skewer into the first colour and dribble the paint onto the desired area. Push the paint outward towards the lead outline with the pointed end of the skewer. Clean the skewer with a paper towel between different colour applications. Use the blunt end of the skewer to fill in larger areas. A dropper is also effective for filling in very large areas.

Glass paint will eventually peal if applied to a surface that is used extensively. Solve this problem by turning over the glass top so that the painted design shows through, but the smooth upper surface can be cleaned. (See page 54 for instructions.)

PAINT – QUICK AND EASY

Many cosmetics and confectionery companies use sturdy plastic containers for gift presentations of soap or chocolate. Keep these and decorate them with glass paint. Decorated, such a container does not need anything in it to make a pretty and useful gift. See page 36 for instructions.

Lead tape

The 10 m rolls of lead tape are available in 9 mm, 6 mm and 3 mm widths. The popular 3 mm wide lead tape has a groove for cutting in half, giving you 20 m of lead. Peel off the paper backing, paste the lead strips in the desired position and rub down firmly with the plastic rod included in the packet. Make sure there are no gaps where lines meet or intersect by pressing the tape ends or overlapping sections firmly together with the rod.

Lead tape is suitable for larger designs and can be moulded to suit specific designs. It can also be successfully combined with silver liquid lead outliner.

Stained-glass paint

Various kinds of glass paint are available. Some kinds can be applied in several layers, while with others, a second layer will cause the first layer to flake. If the article to be painted is going to be exposed to strong sunlight, use a stronger kind of glass paint.

Cans

The tin-coloured inside of cooldrink and beer cans provide a lovely surface for glass painting. The effect of the glass paint is particularly attractive and it is easy to shape and bend the can. Cut open a can as follows:

Pierce a hole close to the top edge of the can with a sharp object such as an awl, jiggle the ends of a pair of scissors through the hole and cut off the top. Cut the can in half lengthwise right to the bottom, twist the scissors and cut off the bottom. Flatten out the strip of tin.

12

Basic Method for Glass Painting

1. Draw the design clearly with a pencil or black felt-tipped pen onto white paper. Place the design under a transparent surface for tracing, or transfer it to an opaque surface with the aid of tracing paper. If you are working on a curved material, lightly flatten it and attach it to a table or other flat surface with sticky tape to prevent the glass paint from spreading over the lead outlines.

2. Trace all the outlines of the design with liquid lead, making sure there are no gaps between the lines. Leave to dry.

3. Dip the wooden skewer into the first glass paint colour and allow the paint to drip into the desired area. Push the glass paint outward towards the lead outline. Continue in this way until the entire area is covered. Complete all areas to be painted in that colour. Clean the skewer with a paper towel and repeat the process with the other colours until all the areas are filled with glass paint.

PAINT – QUICK AND EASY

Canned Frame

When I cut open my first cooldrink can I was pleasantly surprised to find that the inside of these cans have a beautifully finished smooth surface which is just right for decorating with glass paint. With a little imagination you can transform cooldrink and beer cans into the prettiest frame for a photograph or mirror, or into containers, fridge magnets, earrings or whatever else you fancy. Encourage everybody you know to keep their empty cans for you so that you always have a good supply, and experiment to your heart's content: the possibilities are endless. Five tin strips are used for this frame. Use more tin strips for a larger frame.

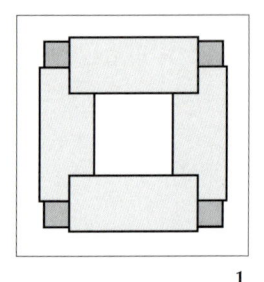

1

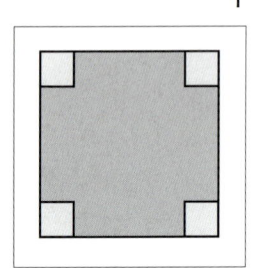

2

Sketch 1 shows you how to glue the tin strips into position, and sketch 2 shows you how to solve the problem in the corners by pasting tin squares, slightly bigger than the cut-out corners of the first cardboard square, onto the second cardboard square

1 Draw a 11x11 cm square in the centre of one of the cardboard squares. Cut it out with a craft knife to leave a frame.

2 Cut open the cooldrink cans as explained on page 12 and flatten them out with the inside facing up.

3 Apply contact adhesive to the coloured sides of two tin strips and to two opposite sides of the cardboard frame. Glue the tin strips onto the glued frame. The tin should overlap the cardboard by about 4 mm on either side. Repeat with the other sides of the frame (*see* sketch 1 on the left).

4 With a craft knife, cut out the four square cardboard corners. Apply glue to the outer edges of the cardboard, fold over the tin overlaps and press it down. Use the pliers if necessary to neatly flatten the edge.

5 Make a diagonal cut in each corner of the inner edge, apply glue to the cardboard and fold over the tin overlap.

6 Cut 4x4 cm squares from the remaining tin strip; glue them onto the corners of the second cardboard square (*see* sketch 2).

7 Punch two holes through the top edge of this cardboard square, thread some thin string through and tie it at the back (to hang the frame). Paste the mirror in the centre of the cardboard. Apply glue to the back of the tin-covered frame and paste it onto the cardboard square, framing the mirror.

8 Draw your design onto the tin frame with a water-based felt-tipped pen. Complete the design with glass paint, using the basic method described on page 13. Leave to dry and glue coloured plastic stones in position.

You will need

2 squares of stiff cardboard (25x25 cm); craft knife; ruler; 5 cooldrink cans; awl (or sharp object); pointed scissors; strong contact adhesive; pliers; 12x12 cm mirror; thin string; water-based felt-tipped pen; black liquid lead outliner; glass paint in different colours; wooden skewer; paper towels; coloured plastic stones

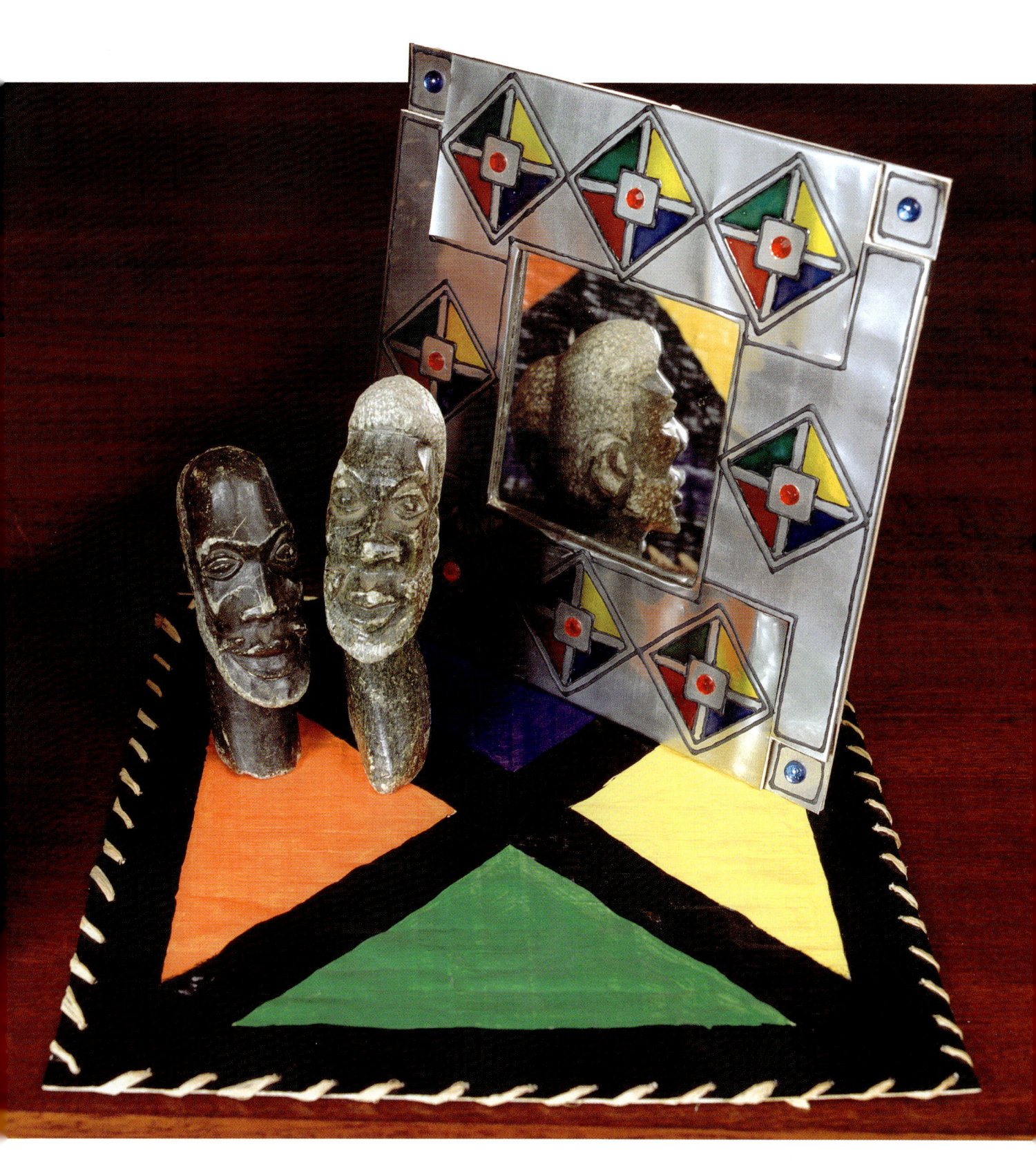

GLASS PAINT

16

GLASS PAINT

A Parrot for the Fridge

This parrot was created to help me deal with my frustration with piles of notices and notes, often spattered with food, scattered around the kitchen. It is so easy to cut out the tin strips from a cooldrink can to any required shape, so have fun making this fridge magnet or whatever other shape you fancy. The parrot is perfect for keeping reminders in a prominent place or for keeping an eye on your shopping list. Do your bit by recycling cooldrink cans, invest in some glass paint, and in no time you will be able to show off your very own parrot perched on its very own magnetic branch.

1 Cut open the cooldrink can as described on page 12 and flatten out the strip of tin. With a felt-tipped pen, draw a parrot without claws on the tin-coloured surface; cut out along the outline.

2 Place the tin parrot on the cardboard and, with an empty ballpoint pen or other suitable object with a rounded point, emboss feathers and other details on the tail and body.

3 Apply lead and glass paint according to the basic method described on page 13.

4 Draw six leaves and two claws on the remaining tin, emboss for texture, cut out and complete with lead and glass paint. Allow everything to dry thoroughly.

5 Glue the strip magnet onto the front part of the parrot where the claws would normally be when it's perched on a branch.

6 Bend the claws slightly; glue onto the strip magnet so that it looks as if the parrot is perched on a branch. Paste leaves into position on either side of the parrot. Leave glue to dry thoroughly before using your fridge magnet.

You will need

1 cooldrink can; awl or sharp object; pointed scissors or all-purpose scissors; water-based felt-tipped pen; empty ballpoint pen; piece of cardboard; liquid lead outliner; glass paint in different colours; wooden skewer; paper towels; strong contact adhesive; 2x12 cm strip magnets

The soft tin of a cooldrink can is ideal for cutting out different shapes, and for embossing additional detail to achieve a realistic finish.

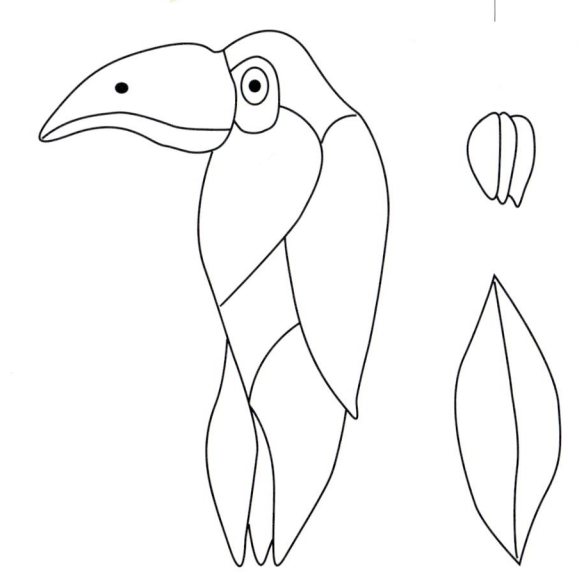

PAINT – QUICK AND EASY

Fleur-de-loo

The tubular middle section of a plastic cooldrink bottle worked beautifully as a candleholder in the shape of an Arum Lily, and when I decided to extend the fleur-de-lis theme in the guest toilet, a candle-holder made with the same method seemed to be just what I needed. Without my consciously planning it, the candleholder doubles as a perfect container for the room freshener (which never seemed able to stay upright). Now, when guests arrive for dinner, it undergoes a transformation and sets the mood as a fleur-de-lis candle! Stickers on the mirror and tiles take the theme further, while the toilet mats and window drapes stamped with fabric painted motifs in the same theme add the final touch (see page 122).

The stickers on the mirror extend the fleur-de-lis theme and also look attractive on the white tiles. With textile paint, stamp the same design onto a white cotton strip stitched onto a white guest towel (see page 122).

The deep-etched picture on the right clearly shows the screw-top section comprising the bottom of the candle holder and the base of the fleur-de-lis design.

1 Enlarge the fleur-de-lis design on page 122 on paper to measure 28x28 cm; cut out.

2 Cut out the base and turn the cooldrink bottle upside down with the screw-top part at the bottom. Lightly paste the design onto the bottle with adhesive tape and trace its outlines onto the bottle with a felt-tipped pen; draw a horizontal line on the back of the bottle, 5 cm from the end of the screw-top part. Cut out along the felt-tipped pen lines.

3 Paint the entire surface with a broad brush with blue glass paint. Leave to dry and repeat until the paint appears opaque.

4 Apply adhesive lead all around the outer edge and front following the design outlines and press down well, or use silver outliner as an alternative.

5 Camouflage the screw-top part by wrapping adhesive lead around it, or cut the same design (10 cm) from the left-over plastic, paint it blue and paste it onto the front.

6 Use double-sided adhesive tape to secure your fleur-de-lis candle into position. When using a candle with dripping wax always make sure it is in a safe place.

7 Follow the steps described for Decorative Stickers on page 20, but using the smaller fleur-de-lis design, to extend the theme. Use these stickers as desired to decorate the mirror and wall tiles.

You will need

fleur-de-lis design;
water-based felt-tipped pen;
2 litre plastic cooldrink bottle;
adhesive tape; pointed scissors;
candle; broad, soft brush;
blue glass paint;
3 mm adhesive lead or
silver liquid lead outliner

18

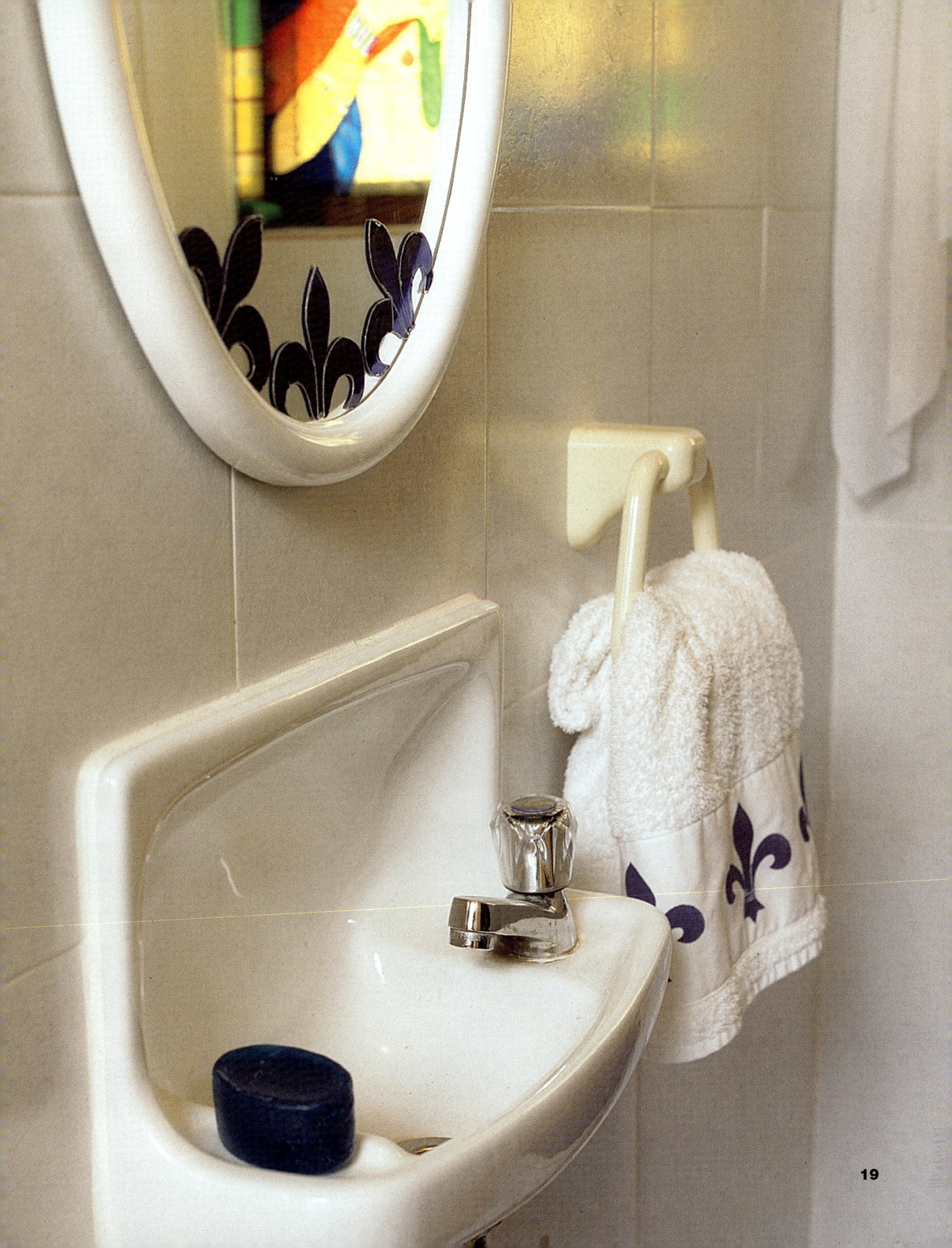

PAINT – QUICK AND EASY

Decorative Stickers

When one of our guests recently walked right into our closed glass sliding doors, we knew we had to do something urgently to prevent another such accident. This is how our decorative stickers originated and since then they adorn not only the sliding doors but anything from tumblers and flutes to tiles, mirrors and windows. Around Christmas and Easter, decorate windows facing the street with theme stickers. Remove the festive designs after the event and stick them onto wax paper to preserve them. Glass paint cannot be washed and so cannot be applied directly to flutes and tumblers. These stickers are ideal for decorating glasses of any shape for special occasions such as birthdays or Valentine's Day. And you can use them again if you peel them off after the event and stick them onto wax paper.

Glass stickers are most versatile and can serve as decoration on their own, as can be seen on the glass panels of this lovely wooden door, or they can be used to reinforce a festive or special theme.

1 Draw the design onto the paper side of the adhesive plastic. Use adhesive tape and lightly attach the adhesive plastic to a flat surface or table with the design in position underneath; trace all the outlines of the design with liquid lead.

2 Complete the designs with glass paint as described on page 13.

3 Cut out each design along its outer edge, carefully peel off the paper backing and use on the surface of your choice.

You will need

assorted designs; black felt-tipped pen; transparent adhesive plastic; adhesive tape; black liquid lead outliner; glass paint in different colours; wooden skewer; paper towels; pointed scissors

20

21

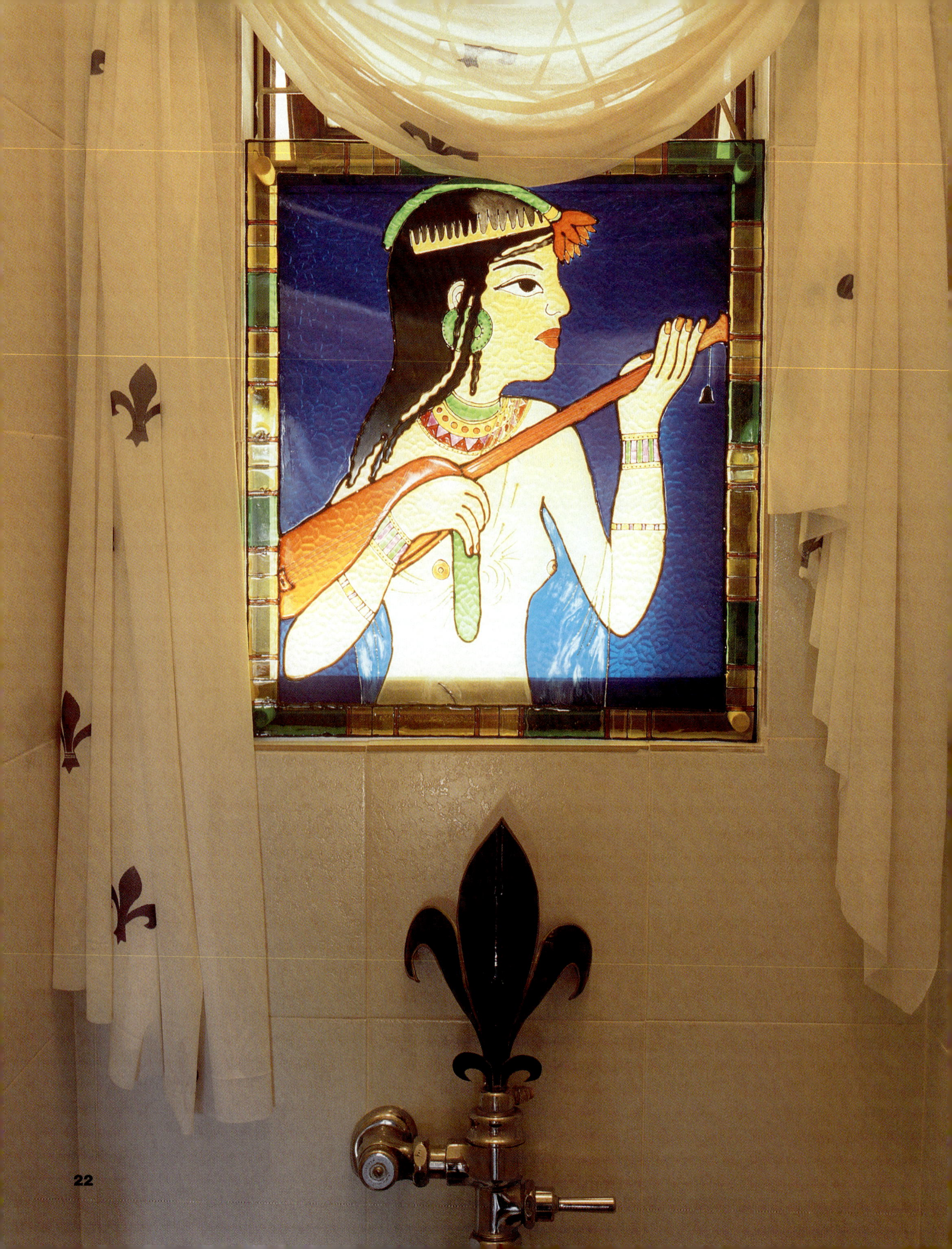

GLASS PAINT

Egyptian Queen

It is understandable that a toilet window cannot be transparent, but does it really have to be so unattractive? After much thought on how to give the window of the guest toilet a facelift, I decided to decorate a perspex panel with glass paint and to place it in front of the window. With the light coming from the back this ugly window now forms a colourful focal point in the toilet and guests like to imagine they are Pharaoh on his throne! The advantage of the perspex panel is that the window does not have to be removed. You can screw the perspex panel onto the window frame or paste it onto the window inside the frame with double-sided tape.

You will need

transparent perspex, 3 mm thick; white paper; felt-tipped pen; design; black and silver lead outliners; glass paint in different colours, as well as 'Opale Scent' (optional); wooden skewer; paper towels; screws or double-sided tape

3 Optional: Apply 'Opale Scent' to selected parts of the design. It is a pearl-finish glass paint which can be mixed with any other colour or applied as a final finish over another colour for a lovely, pearly effect. It is particularly effective on the Egyptian queen's transparent cloak.

4 Drill a hole in each corner of the perspex and screw the decorated panel onto the window frame, or attach it to the glass inside the frame with double-sided tape.

1 Measure the window frame and have the perspex panel cut slightly smaller so that it fits on or into the window frame, depending on how you want to attach it.

2 Enlarge your design on white paper (use a photocopier if available, or use the block method). Place the enlarged design on a flat surface or a table and place the perspex in position over the design. With liquid lead, trace the lines of the design onto the perspex. Complete the design with glass paint using the basic method described on page 13. Leave the paint to dry thoroughly.

A perspex panel covering the bottom part of the window only, decorated with a simple design, can look equally effective. Combine this with a matching blind which can be drawn right down to the perspex strip.

23

PAINT – QUICK AND EASY

Make-up Tin

Making this tin box requires a little more effort than the other tin objects, but anyone who tackles this project will agree that the end product is well worth the effort. The tin strips are joined with ceramic clay and a mirror in the lid makes it even more useful. I use the container for my make-up but you can use it as a trinket box or for any other purpose. Enjoy your inventiveness every time you open the box and are reminded that it started out as a humble cooldrink can!

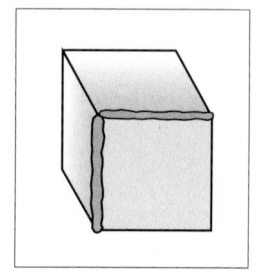

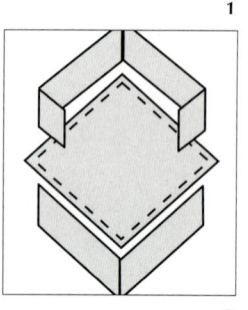

1

2

In sketch 1 you can see how the folded side strips are attached to the bottom square with the clay rolls. Sketch 2 shows how the inner fitting of the lid is put together and glued to the flat part of the lid.

1 Cut open all four cans as described on page 12, and flatten out the tin strips. Measure and cut the following: Two strips of 15x7,5 cm for the sides of the tin and one square strip of 7,5x7,5 cm for the base. Place a ruler in the centre of each long strip; bend the strip at a 90 degree angle so that each strip forms two square sides.

2 Knead the ceramic clay in equal parts until it is even coloured. Roll the clay to form long, thin rolls and place on wax paper ready for use.

3 Place the base square, coloured side up, on wax paper; press a piece of rolled-out clay onto two sides that form a 90 degree angle. Attach one folded side strip on the base square with the clay, pressing the clay onto the side-strip from the inside. Repeat with the other side strip on the other two sides. Now attach the two side strips with rolled-out clay from the inside. Decorate all four corners on the outside, as well as the bottom and top edges with rolled-out clay.

4 Cut two tin squares for the lid, one of 7,5x 7,5 cm and one of 9,5x9,5 cm. Cut out a 5x5 cm square from the centre of the larger square to form a frame.

5 Apply glue to the outside edge of the mirror (reflecting side facing up) and glue the coloured side of the tin frame onto it. Wipe away excess glue. Make diagonal slits in the outer corners of the tin frame that extend beyond the mirror (up against the mirror); apply glue to the tin edges, fold them around the edge of the mirror and paste down. Apply glue to the tin-coloured side of the smaller square and paste the 'framed' mirror onto it.

6 Cut two 16x 2 cm tin strips for the inside fitting of the lid. Bend each strip at a 90 degree angle in the middle and about 10 mm from each end. Glue them together, their ends overlapping slightly to form a square slightly smaller than the square of the container.

7 Apply strong contact adhesive to the bottom edge of the lid fitting and glue it into position on the painted side of the lid by pressing down. Make sure the lid fits neatly into the container part; and adjust if necessary before the glue has dried completely. Decorate the lid around the mirror and outer edge with strips of rolled-out clay. Leave the clay to harden and carefully paint all the clay parts with silver enamel paint. Clean the brush with turpentine while you wait for the enamel paint to dry.

24

GLASS PAINT

8 Transfer your glass paint design onto the sides of the tin and use the basic method described on page 13 to complete the design with lead and glass paint. First complete all the liquid lead lines, leave to dry completely and fill in the glass paint on one side only. Leave to dry, turn the tin onto the next side; continue decorating in this way. This will prevent the paint from spreading over the lead lines.

You will need

4 cooldrink cans; awl or sharp object; pointed scissors; 7,5 cm square mirror; strong contact adhesive; ceramic clay; wax paper; silver enamel paint; fine brush; turpentine; silver liquid lead outliner; glass paint; paper towels

25

26

GLASS PAINT

Butterfly Mobile

I mentioned the versatility of the plastic of cooldrink containers in the Introduction. These butterflies were the first design I cut out from cooldrink bottle plastic and decorated with glass paint years ago. I made big ones and small ones and combined different sizes to serve as earrings, hung them on my ears and even wore one pinned to my shoulder! Let these splashes of colour flutter from a mobile, or stick attach them separately to a window-pane or even a mirror. Their display of colour above a cot is sure to fascinate any baby.

1 Cut out the smooth middle section of the plastic cooldrink bottle and carefully flatten it out to form a strip. Measure and cut out squares of different sizes. I used squares of 13x13 cm, 11x11 cm, and 10x10 cm.

2 Copy the butterfly onto white paper slightly smaller than each plastic square and attach the paper to the inside of the plastic with adhesive tape. Using thumb tacks in the corners of the plastic square, carefully attach it to an old bread board to ensure that the glass paint does not run over the lead outlines because of the curved shape of the plastic.

3 Complete each butterfly with liquid lead and glass paint using the basic method described on page 13, and leave to dry.

4 Remove the plastic square from the bread board; cut out the butterfly along its outline, taking care not to cut through the lead.

5 Heat the sharp point of the safety pin over a candle flame and press two holes into the head section of each butterfly. Cut 10 cm of thin silver wire and insert the two ends through these holes to form the butterfly's feelers. Twist together the two ends of the wire on the other side and glue into position if necessary. Bend or curl the ends of the wire feelers as desired.

6 Decide beforehand how you are going to arrange the butterflies. Use the heated point of a safety pin and make small holes in the wings and thread strong cotton or nylon fishing line through the holes. Combine with small beads if you wish. Do not hang anything with beads within reach of a baby.

You will need

plastic cooldrink bottle; pointed scissors; white paper; pencil; adhesive tape; bread board; thumb tacks; black liquid lead; glass paint in different colours; wooden skewer; paper towels; candle; safety pin; thin silver wire; strong thread or fishing line; beads

PAINT – QUICK AND EASY

Romantic Roses

I discovered quite by accident that heat makes the plastic of cooldrink containers curl most attractively. The resulting curly shapes are ideal for making small rose buds. Besides making my own curly jewellery, I have since used these roses on anything from hair combs, to candleholders and table-napkin rings. A rose theme is suitable for many romantic or other special occasions, such as Valentine's Day, a wedding anniversary or Mother's Day. Decorative stickers with a rose design look beautiful on champagne flutes, and stamping with fabric paint can transform an old sheet into a lovely tablecloth and table napkins. Make your own stamp as described on page 66 and follow the instructions on page 125 for making and decorating a tablecloth and napkins.

You will need

1 plastic cooldrink container;
pointed scissors; pointed pliers;
candle; red and green glass paint;
broad, soft brush;
acetone or thinners;
strong, colourless contact adhesive

You can use the same basic rose design for both the decorative stickers and the stamp used to decorate the table cloth and table napkins.

1. Cut off the top and bottom of the cooldrink container and cut the centre part in half from top to bottom, flattening it out into broad strip. Cut lengthwise into one narrow strip measuring 20x4 cm for the base of the napkin ring, two strips measuring 20x2 cm, and one measuring 10x1 cm for the roses. Cut short notches 2 cm apart into one side of each rose strip. Slightly round all sharp corners.

2. Roll up the first rose strip, tightly pinch the uncut side with the pointed pliers or scissors and carefully turn the side with the notches over a candle flame to make it curl. Leave to cool slightly then loosen the roll a little. Heat again to curl more if necessary. Put aside to cool completely. Repeat with the other rose strips.

3. Cut the ends of the strip for the base of the napkin ring to form points, fold the points over each other in a ring shape and repeat the curling process on both sides, retaining the ring shape.

4. Place the curled shapes on wax paper and paint the ring base with green and the roses with red glass paint. Use a soft brush to reach into all the corners and make sure that the glass paint covers all surfaces. Turn the shapes over after ten minutes, place on clean wax paper and paint the other side. Leave to dry.

5. Arrange the three roses on the green ring and glue them into position with strong contact adhesive. Leave to dry before using.

6. Make decorative stickers with a rose design as described on page 20 and use them to decorate champagne flutes. Remove after using, stick them onto wax paper and store until the next special occasion.

28

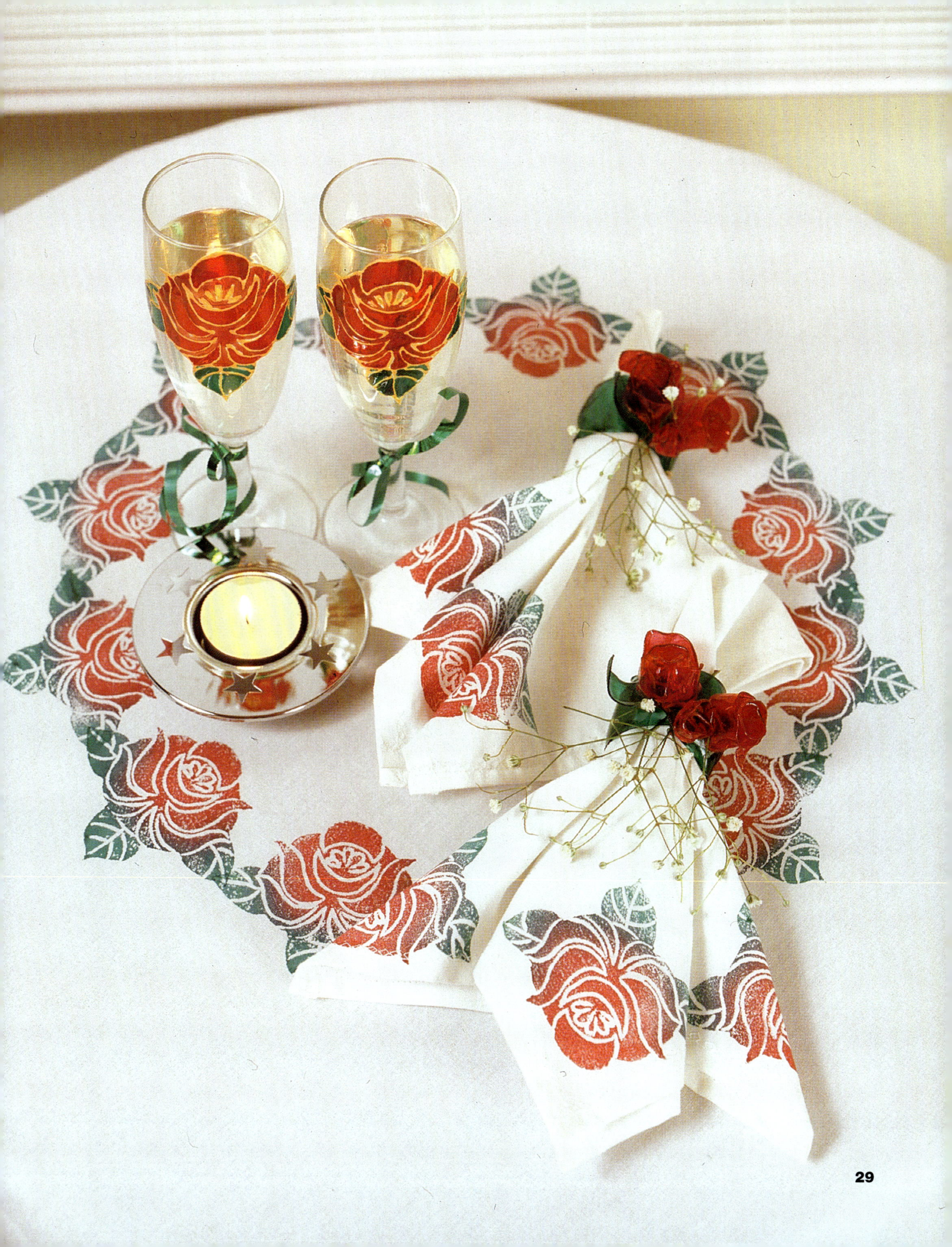

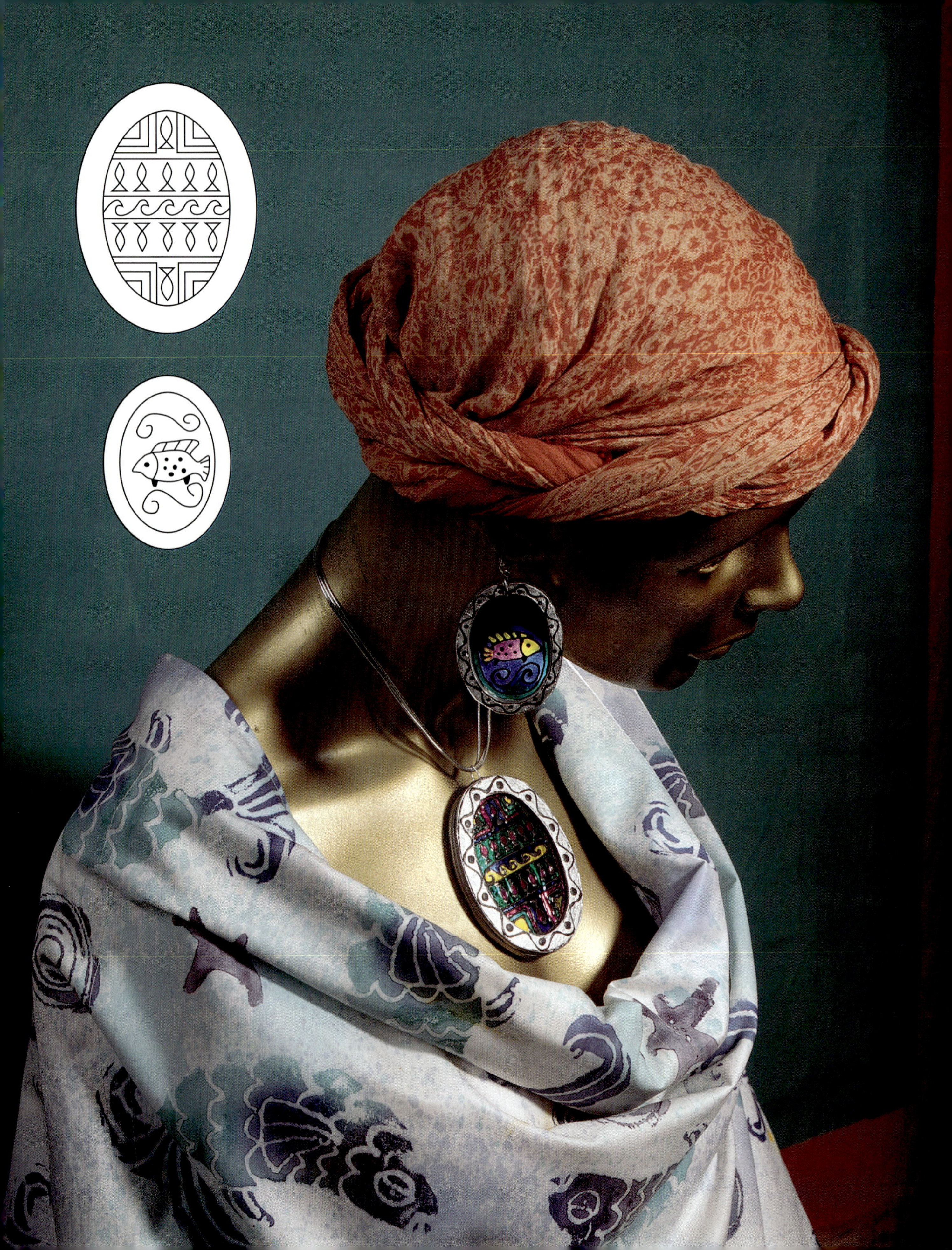

GLASS PAINT

Jewellery Showpieces

In my search for a transparent medium to use for making jewellery, I experimented with transparencies. These earrings with their colourful marine theme have become my favourite earrings. When painted with glass paint, transparencies and cooldrink bottle plastic look like glass. Choose simple designs and decorate the plastic shapes with liquid lead and glass paint in colours of your choice. You can make these earrings and pendant in a jiffy. They always attract attention and cost next to nothing. They also make a delightful gift.

1. From the transparency, cut out two oval shapes 5,5x3 cm for the earrings and one oval 8x5,5 cm for the pendant. Draw simple patterns on white paper and place them under the shapes so that they can be traced.

2. Complete the design with lead and glass paint using the basic method described on page 13. Leave until completely dry.

3. From cardboard or thin cork, cut out two oval shapes 5,5x3 cm for each earring. With a craft knife, cut out the insides to make a double-sided frame measuring 3 mm. Cut out two larger ovals measuring 8x5,5 cm for the pendant, then cut out the inside of one of these to form a frame of 5 mm.

4. Neatly finish off the outer and inner edges of the cardboard or cork frames with adhesive lead. You can also use liquid lead. Paint the frames with silver enamel paint and leave to dry.

5. Apply glue to the insides of each earring frame, and glue each decorated plastic earring shape between two cardboard or cork frames. Glue a piece of thin wire neatly into the top to form a loop for the ringlet and earring hook.

6. Cut out a piece of aluminium foil the same size as the pendant. Glue it onto the one side of the solid cardboard or cork oval, pierce a hole through the top and thread thin wire through to form a loop. Apply glue to the inside of the frame oval and paste it onto the decorated plastic oval. Glue the framed plastic oval onto the aluminium-foil oval.

7. Decorate the frames further with silver liquid lead if you wish. Complete the earrings with a ringlet and earring hook, and the pendant with a thin chain or leather thong.

You will need

white paper; pencil; transparency or cooldrink bottle plastic; pointed scissors; black liquid lead; glass paint in different colours; wooden skewer; paper towels; thick cardboard or cork; craft knife; 3 mm adhesive lead; aluminium foil; strong contact adhesive; thin wire; silver enamel paint; silver liquid lead; 2 earring hooks; 2 small ringlets; thin chain or leather thong

The glass painted design looks as attractive with an aluminium foil backing underneath the plastic (pendant) as it does when left transparent (earrings).

31

PAINT – QUICK AND EASY

Brilliant Jewellery

I like my jewellery for evening wear to match the colour and pattern of my outfit. In the past, this usually meant hunting through many shops, which often also hurt my pocket somewhat. All my frustration came to an end when I discovered what excellent companions aluminium foil and glass paints are. Since then I have been able to proudly show off unique jewellery that matches every outfit. Use these ideas to create your own interesting jewellery to match your outfits. Copy the patterns and designs on your outfits and use them when you design matching jewellery.

Costume jewellery is very popular at the moment, and you don't need much more than a few basic items and imagination to create your own innovative and original pieces.

1 Copy four Paisley shapes measuring 3x2 cm onto stiff cardboard and cut them out around the outer edges.

2 Apply glue to one side of each shape and paste it onto the dull side of the aluminium foil. Leave the glue to dry and neatly cut out the aluminium foil around the cardboard shapes. Use nail scissors for the finer curves and corners. Repeat with the other side of the cardboard shapes.

3 With an empty ballpoint pen emboss patterns on the aluminium foil surface. Remove the ink tube from an old ballpoint pen, press a small piece of rolled-up paper towel into the back of the front metal part and scribble on a piece of paper until it is completely empty. Use this as an embossing tool.

4 Draw lines in silver liquid lead and decorate with glass paint according to your design, as described in the basic method on page 13. Leave to dry and glue coloured stones onto the centre of each shape.

5 Place two Paisley shapes side to side and glue them together to form a brooch by pasting both onto a piece of cardboard in the centre at the back. Glue two coloured stones over the join on the front; outline with silver liquid lead. Attach the brooch clip.

6 Make a multipurpose piece you can use as a pendant as well. Before glueing it to the Paisley shapes, pierce a hole through the cardboard strip used to join the them; insert a ringlet in the hole. Now the 'brooch' can do double duty as a pendant worn on a chain or a thin leather thong around your neck.

7 With a pin, pierce a hole through the top of each earring and complete them by inserting ringlets and earring hooks.

You will need

stiff cardboard; pencil; pointed scissors; contact adhesive; heavy duty aluminium foil; empty ballpoint pen; silver liquid outliner; glass paint; paper towels; coloured stones; ringlets and earring hooks; brooch clip

GLASS PAINT

More Bright Ideas

Cut two simple shapes from a strip of cooldrink can tin (prepared as described on page 12), one slightly larger than the other. Geometric shapes such as squares, diamonds, circles or triangles are particularly suitable. Glue the shapes together with their coloured sides facing and fold over the edges of the larger shape so that there are no sharp ends. Use the basic method on page 13 and decorate both sides with colourful designs in glass paint. If you wish, first emboss with an empty ballpoint pen for an interesting finish. Using a strong needle, pierce a hole through the top and complete the earring with a ringlet and earring hook. Repeat the process for a matching earring.

Following the same steps to make a slightly larger matching pendant.

The butterflies made from cooldrink bottle plastic and decorated with lead and glass paint are not only for a mobile (see page 27) but work equally well as earrings, a brooch or a pendant. Just use your imagination again. Make big ones and little ones, use only one, or make a pair for each ear, or if you dare, let three flutter under one ear. The basic technique remains the same and to attach ringlets and earring hooks in is easy enough.

You can also make your own curly jewellery by curling strips of cooldrink bottle plastic in the heat of a burning candle. This results in interesting irregular shapes which you can decorate with glass paint. Complete with ringlets and earring hooks.

The curly roses described on page 28 look pretty glued to hair clips.

33

PAINT – QUICK AND EASY

Foiled and Framed

Every home has its share of photographs, child art, or prints that lie around begging for a frame – a process usually postponed because of the cost involved. Solve this problem by making your own frames with cardboard, aluminium foil and glass paint. Make the frame a focal point in the room and match it with the colour scheme and design or printed pattern on the curtains or bed cover. The Egyptian theme of this print combines well with the abstract floral design on the blind, which is repeated in the picture frame. The string pasted underneath the flower stems painted on the aluminium foil, the flower buds pasted on top, and the embossed patterns create an attractive three-dimensional effect.

To reinforce the frame, finish it completely but without the string or fishing line for hanging, then glue it onto hardboard cut to size. Screw eyelets into the hardboard and use thin string or fishing line to hang the frame on the wall.

You will need
2 stiff cardboard rectangles (56x50 cm or to suit your requirements); pointed scissors; craft knife; ruler; pencil; thin, soft, thin string; heavy aluminium foil; contact adhesive; 3 mm self-adhesive lead; silver liquid outliner; empty ballpoint pen; black liquid lead outliner; glass paint; wooden skewers; medium brush; paper towels; thin string or fishing line

1 Using a craft knife, cut an inner rectangle out of one of the cardboard rectangles to form a frame with a width of 6 cm.

2 Draw flower stems on the frame according to your design, apply glue to the pencil lines and paste soft, thin string onto these lines. Leave to dry thoroughly.

3 Cut four strips of aluminium foil, 7 cm wide and long enough to cover all four sides of the frame. Apply glue to the surface of the frame and paste the aluminium foil into position as follows: Place the long side of the first foil strip, dull side down, on the inside edge of the frame; with your finger tips, carefully press it down, up against the string. Press the foil over the string and rub it down onto the frame on the other side. This will prevent the foil from tearing. Continue like this until all the strips are glued on. Trim any excess foil that extends beyond the edges.

4 Cut the 3 mm adhesive lead to size; paste a double strip around the outer edge of the frame, and a single strip around the inner edge. If you wish, replace or combine the adhesive lead with silver liquid lead.

5 With an empty ballpoint pen, emboss further floral or other patterns on the the aluminium foil-covered frame.

6 With a medium brush, decorate the frame with glass paint in your chosen colour(s). Paint the stems green.

7 Draw flower and leaf design on the cardboard (6 cm to 9 cm) and cut out. Apply glue to one side and paste onto the dull side of more aluminium foil. Cut out carefully and emboss with an empty ballpoint pen for detail and texture.

GLASS PAINT

8 Decorate all the flowers and leaves with liquid lead and glass paint using the basic method. Leave to dry and glue them onto the frame to go with the stems.

9 With a craft knife, cut out the centre of the other cardboard rectangle, 5 mm smaller all round than the measurements of the photograph or picture you are framing. Glue the photograph or picture into this opening. Paste adhesive lead around the inner frame. Punch two holes close to the top edge (the foil frame will conceal them); thread thin string or fishing line through and tie at the back. Carefully glue the foil frame onto this backing. Allow the glue to dry thoroughly before hanging the framed picture or photograph.

The cut-out flowers and leaves and the string flower stems under the foil create an interesting three-dimensional effect.

35

PAINT – QUICK AND EASY

Trendy Trinket Boxes

I've always enjoyed transforming junk into something useful. For this reason I keep all transparent containers normally used as packaging for soap, chocolate or similar goods. I decorate them with glass paint and use them as gifts in their own right, or to hold small gifts for special people. The containers are also useful as trinket boxes for storing odd articles such as jewellery on your dressing table or pencils on your desk. The potential for patterns and designs is endless and your designs can be made to match any theme. Transform a container with striking giftwrap decorated with a combination of découpage and glass paint. Modge Podge is a ready-made medium for découpage and obtainable from most craft shops.

If you use découpage to decorate a container, make sure the Modge Podge is completely dry before decorating further with glass paint. The pencil box (centre right) has been decorated with découpage; the trinket box far right is an example of a combination of découpage and glass painted geometric patterns.

1 Draw the design to the correct size on paper. With adhesive tape, paste the paper into position under the transparent surface you intend decorating first, and trace the lines with liquid lead outliner. Repeat on the other surfaces, making sure the lead lines are completely dry before turning the container onto a decorated side.

2 Using glass paint in different colours, paint inside the outlines on one side of the container following the basic method on page 13. Leave to dry completely before turning over. The section being painted should always be facing up and remain in this position until the paint is dry to prevent the paint from running over the lead outlines. Paint all the surfaces in this way. Make sure the paint is completely dry before handling the container.

3 Découpage: Cut out small motifs from the giftwrap. Use a small sponge and cover the entire outer surface of the container evenly with Modge Podge. Place the cut-out motifs in position on the wet surface and cover them with Modge Podge as well. Leave to dry. Fill in the areas between the designs with liquid lead and glass paint by using the basic method, completing one side at a time as explained before. Match the patterns and colours of the glass paint with the giftwrap-découpage.

36

GLASS PAINT

You will need
empty plastic or perspex containers;
adhesive tape; black liquid lead;
glass paint; wooden skewer;
paper towels;
for découpage: giftwrap;
scissors; soft sponge;
Modge Podge

37

PAINT – QUICK AND EASY

Contained in Colour

*While preparing a course in glass painting for school children,
I decided to let them make perspex containers because perspex does not break easily.
The children were allowed to choose their own themes and produced charming marine
scenes, galaxies and floral designs. For my container I chose friendly, colourful suns.
Like the make-up tin, this container is also put together with ceramic clay.
The square mirror in the centre is not only useful but also reflects
the glass painted designs on the sides of the container.
The container makes a beautiful gift for old or young,
and is surprisingly easy to make.*

Sketch 1 shows how the first two sides are attached to the mirror at a 90 degree angle with rolls of clay.

In sketch 2 you can see how the corners are joined by carefully pressing ceramic clay from the inside to the outside with beads pressed into corners at the top to finish off.

Sketch 3 shows the container with al sides in position. You can now use rolls and balls of clay for further decoration.

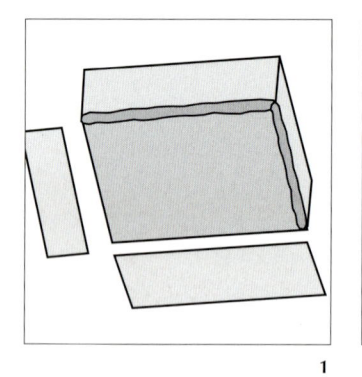

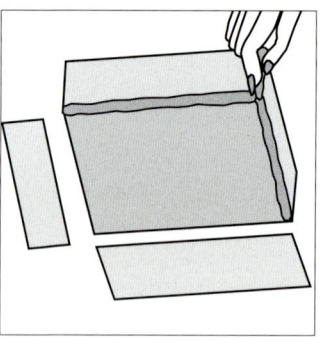

1

2

3

1. Draw the design to the correct size, place it under a perspex rectangle and trace the outlines with liquid lead outliner. Repeat with the other three rectangles. Leave to dry.

2. Use the basic method on page 13 for filling in with glass paint and leave to dry.

3. Knead together two equal parts of ceramic clay until you have one colour. Roll the clay to form long, thin rolls and place on wax paper. Lightly press the rolled-out clay onto two edges of the mirror, forming a 90 degree angle. Place two perspex rectangles, with the painted design on the outside, upright on the clay so that the two short ends form a 90 degree angle. Fix the clay to the inside of the perspex. Join the short ends with roll of clay, pressing it into position from the inside to the outside. Repeat with the other rectangles, making sure all the corners are joined with clay. The clay automatically hardens within an hour owing to a chemical reaction.

4. Decorate further with rolls and balls of clay around the edges and in the joins. Press small beads into the clay in the corners for a final touch if you wish.

5. Wait for the ceramic clay to dry completely before carefully painting the hardened clay with gold acrylic paint.

38

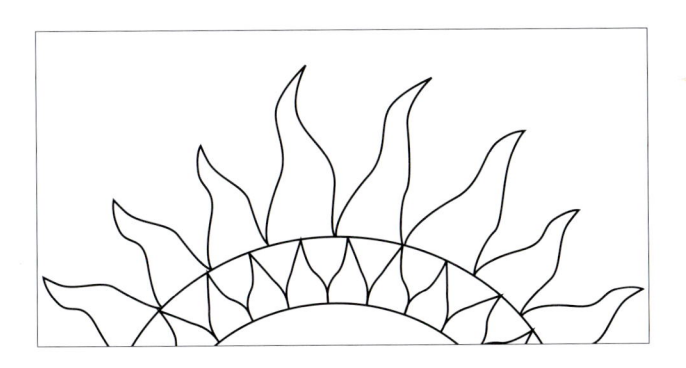

GLASS PAINT

You will need
4 perspex rectangles (10,5x4,5 cm);
gold or black liquid outliner;
glass paint; wooden skewer;
paper towels; 10,5x10, 5 cm square
mirror; ceramic clay;
beads (optional);
gold acrylic paint

39

PAINT – QUICK AND EASY

The Mirror is a Frame

Have you ever considered using a mirror as a frame for a photograph? One morning my 11-year-old daughter and I experimented with various household cleansers to clear a circle from the back of a mirror. Muscle cramps in our hands eventually helped us think of covering the end of an electric beater with fine steel wool and then we managed to make our circle in a flash. (You could use any other shape.) We decorated the front of the mirror with silver liquid outliner and glass paint and pasted the photograph behind the transparent circle. The glass paint takes on a lovely glossy appearance owing to the mirror shining through.

This idea has several possibilities: Make a large family mirror and write each person's name and date of birth under the photograph with lead outliner. You don't have to limit this idea only to photographs. Rub away areas around the edge of a large mirror, resembling a frame. Instead of photographs, paste fabric that matches the curtains in the room over the clear areas. Use your imagination and make something really worthwhile.

These mirror frames have been decorated with a simple circle and square design. Keep the frame design interesting, but avoid a design that will overpower the photograph.

1 Decide on the size and shape of the area(s) you wish to make transparent, turn the mirror around, and mark the area(s) lightly with a pencil. Dip a piece of steel wool in thinners or Brasso and scour in circular movements until the glass shines through. To make things easier, use an electric beater with steel wool wrapped around the end. Apply more thinners or Brasso at regular intervals and wipe the surface with paper towels so that you can see how you are progressing.

2 Draw the design on the front of the mirror with a felt-tipped pen. Use the basic method described on page 13 to decorate the 'frame' with glass paint. Leave to dry.

3 Attach the photograph to the back of the mirror so that it is visible through the transparent glass area. Use adhesive tape so that it can be moved if necessary. Cut a piece of felt the same size as the mirror and paste it onto the back over the photograph.

4 Cut a piece of stiff cardboard large enough for the size of the mirror to serve as a stand. Make a small fold at one end of the cardboard and glue it to the mirror frame, centred about one-third from the top. Use double-sided tape to hang it on a wall.

GLASS PAINT

You will need
mirror; pencil; thinners or Brasso; fine steel wool; water-based felt-tipped pen (pale colour); silver liquid lead outliner; glass paint; wooden skewer; paper towels; adhesive tape; strong contact adhesive; felt; stiff cardboard; double-sided tape

Do not be tempted to use coarse steel wool or sandpaper to hurry the scouring process at the back of the mirror. This will scratch the glass which, in turn, will make the photograph look dull.

41

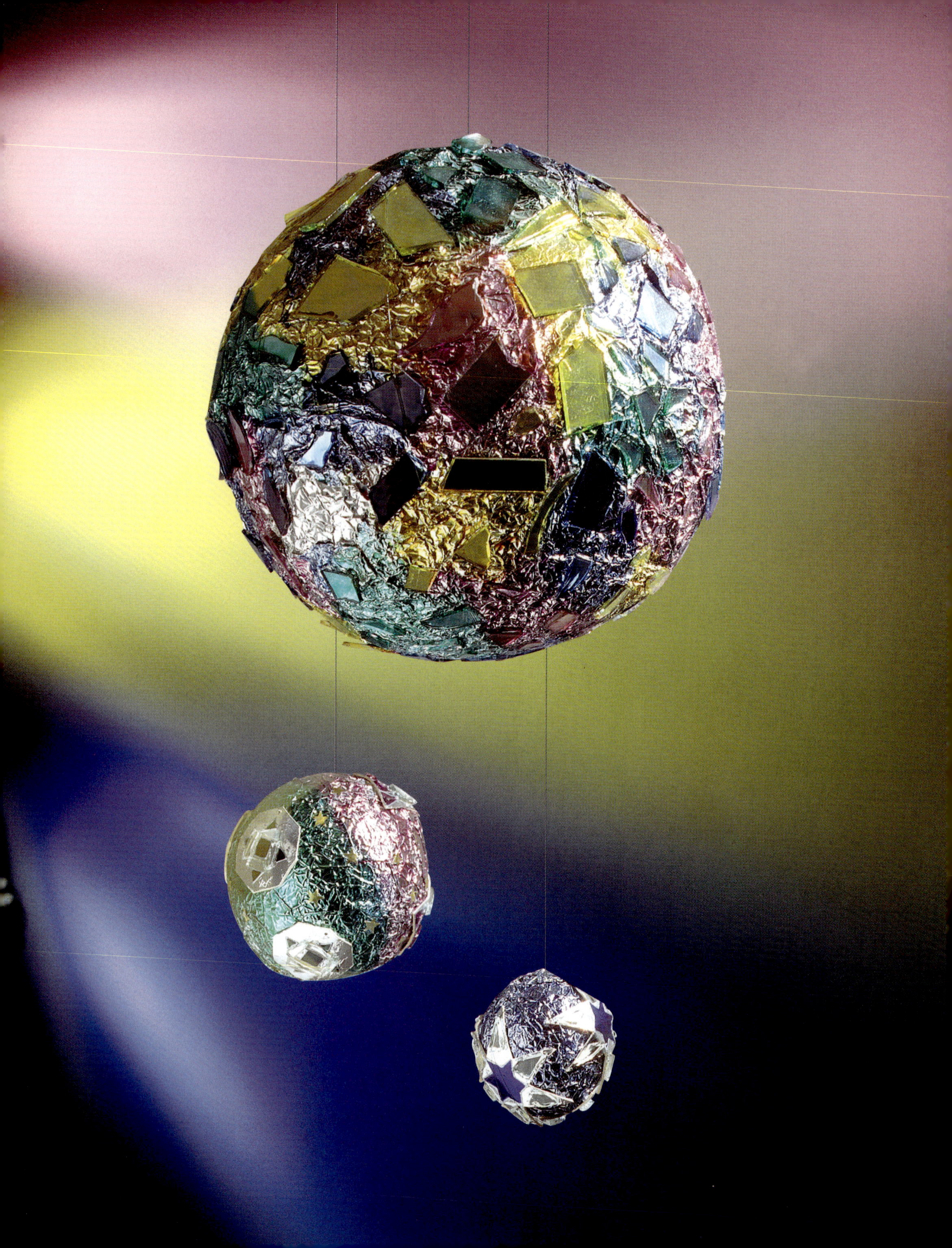

GLASS PAINT

Disco Balls

Fundraising is a necessity at most schools today and a disco evening is always a popular choice. Rather than hiring disco lights for a recent fundraising event, I decided to use festive homemade balls instead. What began as an inexpensive inflatable ball wrapped in aluminium foil grew in something that took everyone's breath away. The balls whirl around automatically and when lights shine on them beautiful darting colour spots are reflected all over the hall creating a perfect party atmosphere!

Another Bright Idea

Use the same combination of aluminium foil and mirror fragments to make unique Christmas decorations. Cut out star, heart, diamond and other shapes from stiff cardboard, cover the shapes on both sides with aluminium foil (dull side on the inside) and glue fragments of glass or mirror to the shapes. Decorate the shapes with liquid lead outliner and glass paint following the basic method. Leave to dry. To hang the decorations on the tree, glue laundry pegs to the back, or thread pieces of string through a hole at the top. Paint and decorate both sides of the shapes if you intend hanging them from a piece of string.

1 Fully inflate the large beach ball and apply glue all over the surface. Place the ball on the dull side of the aluminium foil and wrap it up. Repeat with a second layer of foil to cover the entire ball.

2 Cover the mirror in a towel. Break it up into small pieces with the hammer. It is best to discard the towel afterwards.

3 Apply glue to the back of the mirror fragments and paste them all over the foil-covered ball. Allow the glue to dry.

4 Wrap the fishing line around the entire ball a few times and make a firm knot so that you can attach more fishing line later for hanging up the ball.

5 Balance the ball on an empty tin or container; apply glass paint in different colours to the entire surface, including the mirror fragments. Leave to dry, then paint the other side.

6 Repeat the process with the smaller balls. Tie different lengths of fishing line to the balls and hang them at different heights.

During clean-up operations after the disco, these festive balls were one of the most coveted items among the teenagers who wanted to hang them in their rooms. Remember this next time you are looking for a gift for a teenager.

You will need

1 large and 2 smaller beach balls; heavy aluminium foil; an old mirror; an old towel or cloth; hammer; colourless contact adhesive; fishing line; glass paint; medium paintbrush

PAINT – QUICK AND EASY

Lizard on the Table

The large CD lizard in the photograph on the title page and page 73 was my inspiration for the design on this coffee table. Because I was impatient to see the result, my husband was obliged to leave his briefcase unopened one night and wield a wooden skewer until the early hours of the morning. Afterwards he had to agree that two hands work faster than one!

If it has a glass top, you can choose the best colour and size of design to decorate a coffee table, bedside table or even your diningroom table. Use a motif or pattern from the curtains or rug and repeat it in a suitable size on the glass top. Rhythmic repetition of a motif always results in a pleasing design. Turn over the glass top once the paint is dry, and place it on a suitable base. The painted design shows through from below, while the smooth upper surface can be used without the risk of damaging the paint. An alternative is to place another transparent glass top over the decorated one with washers in-between to lend depth to the design.

All sorts of things can be used as a base for a decorated glass top, including a concrete pillar or a large terracotta pot. Doubling as a base for my table, is this cast iron frame of a dressing table chair, turned upside down.

You will need
glass top (at least 6 mm thick, cut to the desired size); white paper; felt-tipped pen; long ruler; large bottle of black liquid lead outliner; scissors; glass paint; wooden skewer; dropper (optional); paper towels

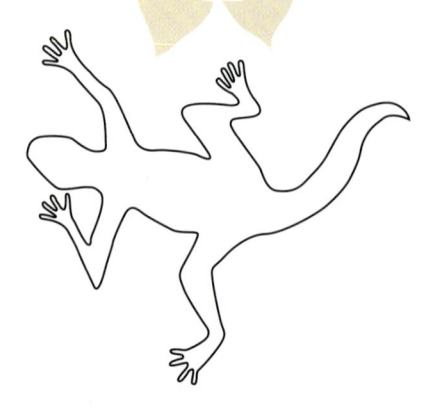

1. Cut a large sheet of white paper the same size as the glass top; on it, draw the design with a felt-tipped pen. Cut the nozzle of the liquid lead outliner shorter so that the hole is larger and you can make thicker lead lines.

2. Trace the design outlines with liquid lead outliner, using a ruler to make sure that long lines are straight. Use the basic method described on page 13 to complete the design with glass paint and leave to dry thoroughly. Use a dropper for filling in large areas. Try not to be impatient. Rather leave the paint to dry over at least two days, especially if you are painting large surfaces.

3. Turn over the decorated glass top, or cover it with another glass top, and place on a suitable base.

GLASS PAINT

Lizard on the Ceiling

I used exactly the same method and a similar lizard design to change an existing light fitting to match the colours and theme of the dining/livingroom.

A perspex circle worked like a charm. Perspex has the appearance of glass, but is lighter and you can drill holes in it, which is very useful. Decorate a perspex circle according to the theme and colours of the diningroom, livingroom or bedroom. Incorporate it into the light fitting as you prefer: Cut a circular opening in the centre of the perspex and attach it to an existing fitting; fit cables or chains to the ceiling and hang the decorated circle under spotlights, or attach a few small lights to the top of the perspex.

First decide how you want to hang the perspex circle and drill holes or cut out the desired areas before you begin decorating with glass paint. Draw the design on white paper, place it under the circle and complete as described for the table top illustrated on the right.

Allow the paint to dry thoroughly before fixing the light fitting in position.

45

PAINT – QUICK AND EASY

Flowery Fan

After having a perspex panel cut for the Egyptian queen in the guest bathroom, I had some perspex left. Usable material left lying around is anathema to me, so I lay awake at night wondering what I could do with it. Until one night when my husband suddenly turned my head to the ceiling. Staring at the ceiling fan I immediately knew what to do.

Ceiling fans are often dull and uninteresting. So why not replace the existing blades of the fan with perspex blades? But first decorate the perspex blades with glass painted designs which match those on the furnishings in the room. Such a unique focal point is sure to turn heads!

You will need
perspex (3 mm thick); drill; white paper; felt-tipped pen; black liquid lead outliner; glass paint; wooden skewer; paper towels

The abstract floral design used on these fan blades works equally well for the unusual blind (instructions on page 84) and were also used in the foil frame.

1. Remove the existing blades of the fan. Make a tracing of one of the blades on paper and cut out the pattern. Take the paper stencil to perspex dealers and ask them to cut four 3 mm thick blades. If they are unable to cut curves, shape the blades yourself with a craft knife and coarse sandpaper. Work carefully and patiently to ensure that the curves are shaped evenly.

2. Drill holes where the blades have to be connected to the base of the fan before you begin the glass painting.

3. Choose a design that will match the theme of the rest of the room. Draw your design on white paper with a black felt-tipped pen and place it under one of the fan blades. Cut the nozzle of the liquid lead outliner shorter to enable you to make thicker lines, if necessary, and trace all the lines onto the perspex with liquid outliner.

4. Complete the design with glass paint as described on page 13. Repeat the process with the other blades

5. Wait until the paint has dried completely before connecting the blades to the base.

6. Optional: Using liquid lead and glass paint, paint a matching design or part of the perspex blade design on the glass lamp shade to complement the blades.

GLASS PAINT

47

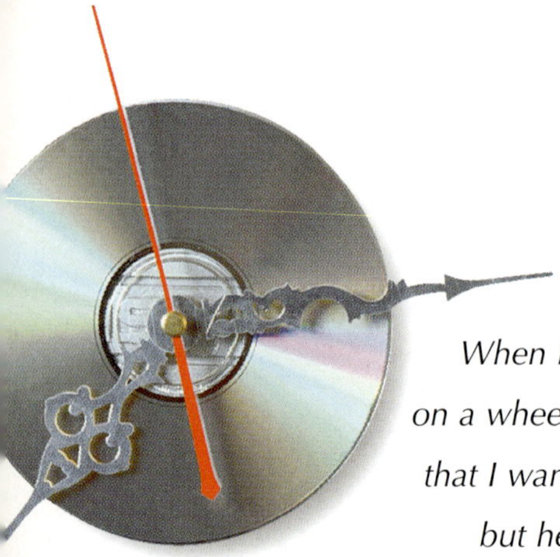

PAINT – QUICK AND EASY

Time Capped

When I asked a car dealer for a hubcap that 'doesn't have to fit on a wheel', he was clearly concerned about my sanity. My explanation that I wanted to make a wall clock only increased his consternation, but he duly went in search of odd hubcaps in his storeroom.

Hubcaps are freely available and an old hubcap is the perfect colour and size for forming the base of an attractive and unusual wall clock. If you make your own clock, you can match the design and colours with the theme of the room in which you intend hanging it. An old CD in the centre behind the hands of the clock adds an interesting touch and makes for a colourful play of light. Glass paint looks particularly attractive on aluminium or aluminium-coloured plastic. Clock mechanisms and hands can be bought at most hardware or craft shops.

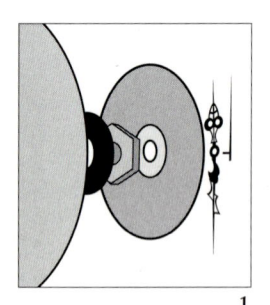

1 Drill a hole in the centre of the hubcap. Make sure that it is large enough for the different parts of the clock mechanism to be fitted comfortably.

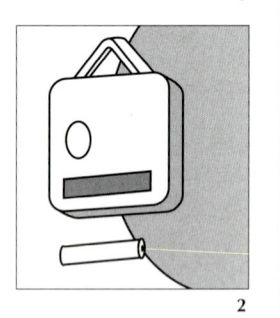

2 Make sure your design provides for or can be adjusted for indicating hours and minutes. Draw the design on the hubcap with a water-based felt-tipped pen.

3 Trace the outlines lines with liquid lead and follow the basic method on page 13 to complete the design with glass paint.

4 Place the CD over the hole you drilled in the centre of the hubcap, with the hands of the clock in the front and the clock mechanism at the back. Fix them in position. The smooth side of the CD shows on the clock face and the label must face the hubcap.

5 Fit a small battery into the clock mechanism, set the time and hang the clock on the wall (fit a suitable hook).

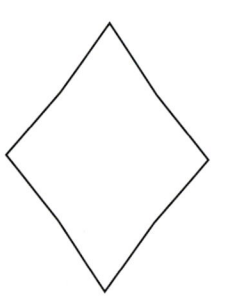

In sketch 1 you can see the sequence for fitting the various parts of the clock and the clock mechanism. Sketch 2 shows the position of the battery.

You will need

hubcap; water-based felt-tipped pen;
silver liquid lead outliner;
red and black glass paint;
wooden skewer; paper towels;
old CD; clock mechanism
and hands; battery

GLASS PAINT

50

GLASS PAINT

Fantasy Lamp

Wire lampshade frames are usually covered with parchment (a white, plastic-like material), and then covered with fabric. Instead of using fabric, I began experimenting with painting directly on the parchment. Bring fantasy characters to life in the nursery or children's room by painting them with glass paint on parchment. You can create a fairytale scene by surrounding a fairytale character with simple flowers, leaves and butterflies. Use glass paint by itself or combine it with giftwrap motifs sealed with Modge Podge (see page 36). Cut out parts of the design separately for a three-dimensional effect. Paint an old lamp base with silver spray-paint as a final touch.

1. Secure the parchment rectangle to a table top or flat surface with adhesive tape to make sure it lies flat and cannot shift around. Use tracing paper to transfer the design onto the parchment.

2. Trace all the outlines with silver liquid lead and leave to dry.

3. Cut motifs from gift wrap and paste them onto the parchment with Modge Podge, creating the planned fairytale scene. Cover the motifs with a layer of Modge Podge; do this in circular movements with your index finger, making sure all the paper edges lie flat. Continue in this way until the whole parchment rectangle is covered with Modge Podge. Leave to dry.

4. Trace all the outlines of the giftwrap motifs with silver liquid lead outliner and leave to dry.

5. With a soft brush, apply glass paint to the background in the colour of your choice, right up to the liquid lead lines. Fill in the colours of the fairytale character with a skewer so that they stand out more solidly.

6. Remove the parchment from the flat service when the paint is dry and cut along the lead outlines at the top and bottom edges. Cut out a section of the wing(s) of the fairy (or do any other cutting work).

7. Punch holes at regular intervals in the short ends of the parchment. Wrap the parchment around the lampshade frame with the ends overlapping slightly; stitch together through the holes with raffia or thick thread.

8. Paint the lamp base with silver spray paint. Leave to dry thoroughly, fit the light bulb and place the lampshade in position.

You will need

white parchment rectangle; tracing paper; silver liquid outliner; giftwrap with suitable motifs; pointed scissors; Modge Podge; damp cloth; glass paint; soft brush; wooden skewer; paper towels; craft knife; awl or sharp object; thick needle; raffia or strong thread; old wire lampshade frame; old lamp base with light bulb; spray paint

This parchment lampshade was made to the same basic method, showing off the cut-out sections to best effect.

PAINT – QUICK AND EASY

Colour me Quickly

One of my children wanted to make bookmarks decorated with glass paint and decided to drip paint on a strip of acetate and then blot it with a second strip so that the paint would spread. This resulted in a colourful bookmark and, inspired, I began using double acetate circles to make a multi-purpose and practical tray lining.

This method has so many other possibilities – photograph frames, coasters, a cover for an ice-bucket or wine-holder ...
If you use white parchment instead of acetate on one side, the colours are even brighter.

The different colours of glass paint flow into each other and form irregular patterns.

You will need

transparent acetate or transparency plastic; scissors; newspaper; skewer; glass paint; paper towels;

Optional: candle; safety pin; raffia; embroidery thread or cord; thick needle

1 Cut out two circles from the acetate to fit neatly into the tray. Place one of the circles on a sheet of newspaper.

2 With a wooden skewer, drip glass paint all over the surface of the circle. Clean the skewer with a paper towel and drip more paint in a different colour in between. Continue in this way until you are satisfied.

3 Carefully place the second circle over the paint-covered circle and press down lightly with your fingers to make the colours flow into each other. Work carefully so that the paint spreads right up to the edges of the circles but not out of the circle. Pull the two circles apart and place on a clean sheet of newspaper, wet sides facing up.

4 Leave the paint to dry slightly (it should be sticky); press the circles together again. The sticky glass paint acts as making the two circles stick together. If you cut and paint neatly, your tray lining will not need further finishing off. If you wish, finish it off with raffia, embroidery thread or cord. Heat the point of a safety pin over a candle flame; make holes all around the edge of the tray lining. With a thick needle, thread raffia, embroidery thread or cord through the holes.

GLASS PAINT

Coasting Along

Somehow I had to combat the constant red-wine stains on my white tablecloth, and the water marks on my wooden side tables. Bearing in mind the fun I had making the tray lining, I found a pile of old transparencies and began playing with patterns and colours. Coasters often look rather dull and uninteresting if one only caters for their practical use. But glasses are transparent, so it is a good idea to make the coasters as bright as possible. A second sheet of transparency plastic over the sheet on which the design is painted will prevent the paint from peeling or rubbing off through use. Make an additional set to give to your hostess next time you are invited to dinner. It is sure to be a much appreciated gift.

1. Draw the design on white paper inside a circle measuring about 6 cm.

2. Place transparency plastic or acetate over the design and trace the circle and all the lines with liquid lead outliner. Repeat with all the coasters you are making. Fill in the colours with glass paint according to the basic method described on page 13; leave to dry slightly (the paint should be sticky).

3. Place a second sheet of transparency or acetate over the decorated circles just before the paint has dried completely; press down firmly but carefully. Cut out the coasters around the outer edge of the black lead lines.

Fruit shapes such as strawberries, grapes, apples, and so on are cheerful motifs for cooldrink tumblers or for informal occasions. Star-shaped coasters with glitter applied over the glass paint will transform a Christmas party into a glittering occasion. Sunflowers or any other floral motifs look striking on a patio or in a sunroom where you often entertain guests.

You will need

transparency plastic or acetate;
white paper; pen;
black liquid lead; glass paint;
pointed scissors

Choose motif for your coasters to match the theme of the occasion: the coasters are made in a jiffy and can form part of the table decorations.

53

PAINT – QUICK AND EASY

Sunshine on my Table

My daughter needed a table for her bedroom, at that stage decorated around a theme of moons and suns. A rickety round wooden table in the storeroom held little promise except for its shape. But with a floor-length tablecloth to hide the ugly legs and a glass top decorated with a happy sun surrounded with stars and moons, the table was saved from becoming firewood and instead became a thing of beauty and the envy of my daughter's friends. After decorating it, I turned over the glass top so that it can be used without my daughter worrying about the paint peeling off. Glass can be cut into almost any shape, it is easy to keep clean, and always looks good. Remember this whenever you are in despair about a table that has lost its good looks.

We stamped a border of gold suns and stars around the edge of the white tablecloth, repeating these designs on the white curtains to match the design on the table.

1 Draw the design on a sheet of white paper (in a circle for a round table), place it in position under the glass top and trace all the lines with gold liquid lead outliner. Leave until completely dry.

2 If the subject lends itself to a glossy appearance, rub gold appliqué glue over the desired areas with your fingers. Leave to dry before the next step.

3 Apply the glass paint according to the basic method described on page 13. Apply the background colour with a soft sponge for a sponged effect. If you prefer a more solid colour effect, use a skewer. Use a dropper to apply paint to larger areas. Make sure the paint is completely dry before proceeding to the next step.

4 Cover the table with a tablecloth that reaches to just above floor level. The tablecloth should preferably be white so that the colours used to decorate the glass top stand out better. Alternatively, use a coloured tablecloth and cover the top with a white cloth circle under the glass top. Carefully turn over the decorated glass top and place it in position on the table.

What you will need

white paper; glass top (6 mm thick and cut to the desired shape); gold liquid lead outliner; gold appliqué glue; glass paint; wooden skewer; dropper; paper towels; soft brush; white tablecloth

54

55

PAINT – QUICK AND EASY

Candles for Africa

To my mind, a candle or two on the table is a must at dinner time. What's more, if your candleholders match the colour scheme and the theme of the diningroom and crockery, they will contribute to the table decorations. The imaginative use of a few empty plastic cooldrink bottles means you won't have to spend a fortune on candleholders and you can afford to change your themes whenever you entertain.

I made these candleholders in next to no time. The geometrical African motifs are a perfect match for the geometrical patterns on the place mats, and the candles look equally good on black and white. A base of cardboard and aluminium foil supports the candleholders. Glass paint tends to run on a curved surface. I solved this problem by painting the design on transparent adhesive plastic and sticking them onto the wide plastic tubes I cut from the cooldrink bottles to serve as candleholders.

You will need

2 litre plastic cooldrink bottle per candleholder; awl or sharp object; scissors; transparent adhesive plastic; black felt-tipped pen; black liquid lead outliner; glass paint; skewer; paper towels; cardboard; aluminium foil; contact adhesive; candle; coloured glass or plastic stones

These African candleholders create a wonderfully informal atmosphere and always look striking, especially offset against black or other earthy colours.

1 With an awl or other sharp object, pierce a hole about 4 cm from the top of the screw top of the plastic cooldrink bottle. Jiggle the scissors into the hole and neatly cut off the top. Repeat at the bottom. You should be left with a wide plastic tube.

2 Using a felt-tipped pen, trace the pattern you have chosen for the border of your candleholder onto the paper side of the adhesive plastic. It is a border pattern, so you must ensure that the two ends will match when you paste the decorated border onto the plastic tube. Flatten out the adhesive plastic and secure lightly to a table or flat surface with adhesive tape.

3 Trace the outlines with liquid lead outliner and fill in with different colours of glass paint as described in the basic method on page 13. Leave to dry thoroughly.

4 Peel off the paper backing of the adhesive plastic and paste the decorated border strip into position around the top edge of the plastic tube you cut from the cooldrink bottle. Cut out the border pattern through the adhesive plastic and the plastic tube taking care not to cut through the lead outliner.

5 Cut out a cardboard circle with diameter 10 cm; with contact adhesive, glue it onto the dull side of aluminium foil. Trim the aluminium foil around the circle. Decorate the border of the aluminium circle with lead outliner and glass paint to match the design on the cooldrink bottle. Leave to dry thoroughly.

6 Glue coloured stones onto the circular base where desired; glue the decorated plastic tube onto the circular base.

7 Insert a candle into the screw-top part of the cooldrink bottle; place it in the decorated tube on the circular base. The screw-top part can be glued into position as well.

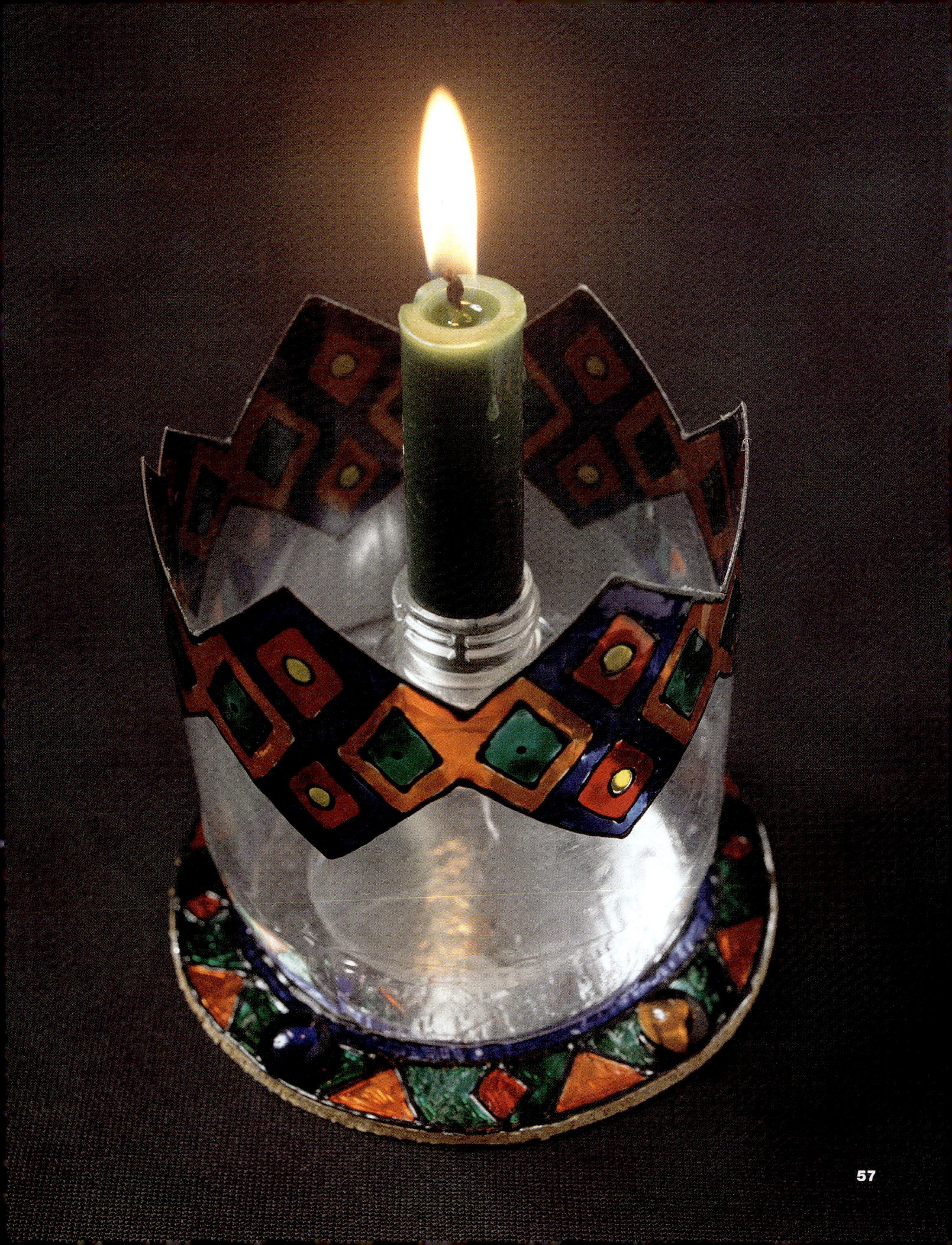

PAINT – QUICK AND EASY

Candle in a Ball

For the stage decor of a school cabaret we had to find a way to ensure that the masses of candles we were using could burn safely throughout the event. At last I had found a practical use for those boring round glass or plastic lamp covers so often found in mass accommodation and bathrooms. We decorated the lamp covers, and placed the burning candles inside, and our candle lamps lit up the stage until the early hours of the morning.

I have since used them often when we entertain outdoors at the pool, where the spherical lamp cover protects a candle flame against even the strongest wind. It can be used equally effectively on the diningroom table or in the bathroom to create a romantic atmosphere.

You will need

spherical glass or plastic lamp cover; self-adhesive plastic; scissors; blue and yellow glass paint; gold liquid lead outliner; thin plastic (such as clingwrap); 2 paper plates; safety pin; gold spray paint; candles

These candle balls occupy a special place in my bathroom where they have a dual function: decorative and romantic.

1 Draw stars on self-adhesive plastic, cut out and paste onto the lamp cover.

2 Pour a small amount of blue glass paint into a paper plate. Crumple the thin plastic into a ball, dip it into the glass paint and sponge all over, covering the entire lamp cover in blue paint. This method creates an attractive texture and prevents the paint from running on the round surface. Always work with small amounts of paint, adding more when necessary. Leave to dry. (Use a hairdryer if you wish to speed up the process, but work carefully.)

3 Use a pin to loosen the points of the plastic stars and carefully peel them off.

4 Crumple a clean piece of plastic; using the same method as above, sponge yellow glass paint onto the white stars left where the plastic shapes covered the surface. Leave to dry. Use gold lead outliner to finish off the stars and to fill in detail on the background.

5 Paint the screw-top and the loose base-fitting with gold spray paint.

6 Rest the closed sphere of the decorated lamp cover on the base and place a candle inside. First fit the candle into the cut-off screw-top part of a plastic cooldrink bottle to keep it from falling over inside the lamp cover.

GLASS PAINT

PAINT – QUICK AND EASY

Tall Lamp with Perspex

A large beach umbrella we bought recently came in a tall box. I couldn't possibly throw away such a lovely strong box and when my eyes fell on the perspex panels left over from my last project, my imagination took off and I visualised the box turned into a lamp. Since we had only white acrylic paint in the house, I had to improvise. I applied white acrylic paint to the box, followed by a strong, geometric design painted in fabric paint in various colours. This turned out to look really striking. I decorated the perspex panels with a similar design in glass paint, cut out corresponding panels from the sides of the box and glued the decorated perspex panels into these openings. Our unusual and proudly displayed lamp attracts so much attention, I am considering patenting it!

Make sure the tubular lamp or bedside lamp that you are using in the lampshade is mounted high enough to allow the light to shine through the perspex panels.

You will need

2 strong boxes (1 square, 1 rectangular); craft knife; steel ruler; white acrylic paint; paint brushes (1 broad, 1 thin); fabric paint; paper towels; 3 mm thick perspex panels; white paper; pencil; black liquid lead; glass paint; skewer; strong colourless contact adhesive; colourless varnish; aluminium foil; bedside lamp or tubular lamp

1 Cut out and remove one side of the square box. Turn it over so that this side is at the bottom. Cut out the narrow ends of the rectangular box and centre one end on top of the square box. Trace the outlines of this end onto the square box and cut along the tracing lines with a craft knife. Push one end of the rectangular box through this hole.

2 Centre a perspex panel lengthwise on a long side of the the rectangular box; trace its outlines with a pencil. Repeat with the other panels; carefully cut along the tracing lines with a craft knife, remove the panels.

3 Paint the inside and outside of the rectangular box and the outside of the square box with white acrylic paint and leave to dry.

4 Draw a design on the outside and top inner edge of the box shape that will match the design on the perspex panels. Use a thin brush and paint the outlines with black fabric paint. Leave to dry and fill in the colours. Clean the brush thoroughly between applications and dry with paper towels.

5 Draw the design for the perspex panels on white paper and place in position under the perspex. Complete with liquid lead and glass paint according to the basic method described on page 13 and leave to dry thoroughly. Repeat with the other perspex panels.

6 Apply strong contact adhesive to the inner edge of a panel opening in the rectangular box and around the edge of the corresponding perspex panel. Carefully place the panel into the opening and hold in position. Make sure it adheres firmly. Leave the glue to dry and repeat with the other panels.

7 Finish off the design by outlining the edge of the perspex panels with black fabric paint. Leave to dry; apply a layer of varnish to all the cardboard parts of the lampshade.

8 Mount a tubular lamp on the inside, or place the decorated lampshade over a discarded bedside lamp.

61

62

PAINT – QUICK
AND EASY

With a pot of paint ...

Fabric paint is an excellent medium for adding new lustre to worn articles such as old sheets, pillow-cases, curtains and tablecloths, or to transform them into blinds, waistcoats, scatter cushions or even chair or duvet covers. So recycling remains the central theme. There are many simple paint techniques and methods, which means anyone can apply paint to fabric.

Fabric paint adds new lustre

PAINT – QUICK AND EASY

Basic Requirements

Thick fabric paint

Fabric paint consists of a thick, transparent, jelly-like base to which colour pigment has been added. If you use large quantities of fabric paint, buy the base in a large container and add the colour pigment yourself.

Liquid fabric paint

Liquid fabric paint is much thinner than ordinary fabric paint and has a water base. Where liquid fabric paint is recommended you may also use silk paint, and in some cases (as with batik) you may use ordinary fabric dye.

Outliner

Fabric paint outliner is useful for adding that final touch to fabric paint projects. It is available in tubes. You can make your own by pouring ordinary thick fabric paint in a plastic bottle with a thin nozzle. Use this to outline your designs. You may also use silk paint outliner with fabric paint. Another option is coloured appliqué glue, which works well for finishing off fabric painted items.

Brushes

With fabric painting, brushes with firm, hard bristles achieve the best results. Buy fine, medium and thick brushes, as well as a fine outline brush for filling in detail. Keep old brushes for working with wax.

Making it easier

If you wish to repeat a pattern, try any of the following to make painting easier.

- Cut out a cardboard shape, place it onto the fabric and draw pencil lines on the fabric around it. Move the shape to the next section and repeat until you have covered the surface in pencil shapes.

- Draw the shapes you wish to paint on the paper backing of self-adhesive plastic and cut out. Peel off the paper backing and paste the stencil onto the fabric. Always paint from the plastic stencil towards the fabric to prevent paint from seeping over the lines of the stencil or running into the area you wish to block out.

Basic Techniques

Freehand painting

There are many ideas for designs to be found on wrapping paper, in magazines, on cards, the patterns on a rug, or even the motifs on your curtains. Enlarge or reduce the design with a photocopier and place it under the fabric you want to paint so that the design shows through. If it does not show through clearly, improvise and make your own 'light table'. Secure the fabric, with the design in position behind it, to a window so that the light shines through the fabric and the design

Ready-made stamps, polystyrene to make your own, brushes, fabric paint, wax, a stamping pad and paper towels are all tools of the trade for fabric painting projects.

FABRIC PAINT

This one-piece mat connecting the shower and the handbasin was decorated by freehand painting. White fabric paint, combined with gold, looks striking and elegant on the cream-coloured cotton fabric.

Hints and Tips

- Always wash new fabric before applying fabric paint, to remove any starch.

- Keep in mind that most kinds of fabric paint have a colourless base and with the exception of white, gold and silver, which are opaque, should only be applied to light-coloured fabric.

- Clean brushes with water between colour applications and dab dry on paper towels.

- Whichever method you use, iron each painted article, or place in a tumbledrier for a few minutes, or blow hot air over it with a hairdrier so that the heat can fix the paint (make it colourfast).

- You can mix any colour with the basic colours – red, yellow and blue. Add white paint for a lighter shade of any colour.

lines are clearly visible. Lightly trace the design with a pencil. Alternatively, divide the design into squares, fold the fabric into the same number of squares; with a pencil, transfer the design to the fabric block by block.

Use a firm brush and apply the fabric paint evenly. Use light or dark colours for a shadow effect and to add greater dimension if you prefer. To add interest and texture, apply a second colour over the first and use a skewer or the back of the paint brush to scratch out detail or patterns in the wet paint.

Starch-masking method

Transfer the design to the fabric and place the fabric on a table or flat surface covered with newspaper. Mix and beat some flour and water to a consistency slightly thicker than pancake batter. Pour into a plastic bottle with a nozzle (for instance an empty tomato sauce or mustard bottle). Carefully squeeze out the starch along the design lines where you want

The starch-masking method is particularly effective for decorating a blind since. With light shining through the masked out sections, from behind, the blind looks like a huge batik.

65

PAINT – QUICK AND EASY

to mask out any colour. Allow to dry and apply fabric paint as desired to areas between the starch lines. Because fabric paint is so thick, it won't run into the starch. Leave the paint to dry and carefully scratch off the starch with a blunt knife or cheese cutter.

Stamping

A large variety of fabric stamps are obtainable from craft shops and are usually sold with a stamping pad. You can use these stamps for printing on virtually anything: walls, cushions, lampshades, T-shirts and other clothing, and even on paper serviettes.

Apply fabric paint in the colours of your choice to the stamping pad, roughly following the shape of the design you intend stamping. To make sure you get this right, paint the different colours onto the stamp with a brush, make a print on the stamping pad and then apply the paint as indicated by the print. Make sure the pad is saturated with paint, dab the stamp into the pad with a pumping action, and check that the surface of the stamp is shiny all over before printing on the fabric. If the motif on the stamp is simple and does not have many grooves, you can eliminate the use of the stamping pad and simply apply the paint to the stamp with a brush.

It is easy to make your own stamps, using household items:

- Using a safety pin heated over a candle-flame, cut out a motif from a **polystyrene tub** and press a small ball of Prestik to the back to hold and handle it.

- Draw simple motifs on an **eraser** and

Keep any polystyrene containers after use (many products come in these containers). You can turn them into unusual stamps quickly and easily and achieve the same results as with the most expensive ready-made stamps. Besides, they enable you to make specific designs for stamping.

66

carve out the surrounding area with a craft knife. You can use a **potato** as well. Wash the potato thoroughly, cut it in half and carve a motif as for the eraser. Dab dry with paper towels before using.

- Draw a motif on stiff cardboard, glue string along the outline and secure Prestik or a cork to the back for holding and handling.

- Mould modelling clay (Plasticine) into the desired shape (for example a fish), flatten one side and draw patterns into the flat surface with a skewer or toothpick. Add pieces of string for additional texture. Flatten the surface again before printing.

- Glue an interestingly shaped leaf onto a piece of cardboard, face down; cut out the cardboard to the shape of the leaf and press a ball of Prestik into the back for holding and handling. The leaf will make a beautiful stamp with its veins showing.

- Make your own **stamping pad**: Glue a layer of sponge, 3 mm thick, onto stiff cardboard with cold glue. Leave the glue to dry before using.

Spraying

Liquid fabric paint or silk paint and an atomiser are used for this technique. An atomiser consists of two metal tubes (one thin and one thick) connected at an angle of 90 degrees. Place the thin tube in the paint and blow through the thicker tube. Hold the opening of the thicker tube over the part of the fabric you want sprayed, about 15 cm from the surface. When you blow through the thick tube, a thin spray of paint emerges from this opening.

This technique is really versatile: Spray different colours in spots or stripes for a colourful effect; mask out alternate areas on the fabric with strips of adhesive tape to create a tartan effect; or stick paper motifs, doilies, leaves, or other objects onto the fabric and spray different colours around them. Spraying can be combined most effectively with stamping or starch masking.

Hint: To prevent spills and to facilitate the blowing action, make a hole in the cap of the paint bottle (or in the cap of a 2-litre milk bottle, which fits on a 50 ml bottle of paint) for the thin tube of the atomiser to fit into.

Shortcut batik

With a pencil, lightly draw the design on thin cotton fabric and place the fabric on a thick layer of newspapers on a flat surface next to the stove or primus stove. Melt $^2/_3$ paraffin wax with $^1/_3$ synthetic bees wax. Test the degree of heat on a scrap of fabric: if the wax is hot enough, it will be absorbed by the fabric immediately. If it is too hot, it will spread too much. Dip a firm, thin brush in the wax and paint a wax outline all along the design lines. Lift the fabric every now and again so that it does not stick to the paper. Place the fabric on a clean layer of newspapers and complete your design by filling in the colours with liquid fabric paint, silk paint or ready-mixed dye. Leave to dry. Heat the wax again, pinch an old sponge with a laundry peg and use this to paint a layer of wax over the whole surface. Crumple up the wax-covered fabric, flatten it out again and apply paint in a dark colour with a broad brush, making sure that it spreads into the cracks. Wipe off any excess paint and leave until completely dry. Place the fabric on a thick layer of newspapers and cover it with a separate sheet of newspaper. Iron over it so that the wax melts and is absorbed by the newspaper. Use clean layers of newspaper and continue ironing until all the wax has been absorbed.

The atomiser which I used for the spraying technique in this book was originally made for potters to lend a soft paint effect to their pottery.

PAINT – QUICK AND EASY

Couch Lizards

The old couches which I had had reupholstered in blue and red were begging for new scatter cushions. The choice of colours was easy, but I wanted cushion covers with an earthy look. So my lizards made their appearance once again. I made my own stamp by cutting out a lizard shape from a polystyrene tub, and used some old table napkins for the front part of the cushion covers. I combined several fabric painting techniques before I was satisfied with the effect and texture.

You will need

old white table napkins or strong cotton squares (40x40 cm); firm, broad brush; fabric paint; adhesive tape; self-adhesive plastic; scissors; glass or mirror square; paper towels; polystyrene tub; candle; safety pin; Prestik; newspapers

The polystyrene stamp I made for the cushions did not have any grooves or fine detail in which the paint could collect, so I applied the paint directly onto the stamp with a brush, without using a stamping pad.

1 For a simple ethnic background design, cut out shapes from adhesive plastic, combine with strips of adhesive tape and paste onto a cotton square. Apply paint in the desired colours; leave to dry. Peel off the adhesive tape and shapes, paint the masked sections in contrasting colours and allow the paint to dry.

2 Using long brush strokes in the desired direction(s), apply dark paint to a glass or mirror square. Cover an area as big as the cotton square. Use the back of the paint brush to scribble patterns matching your theme in the paint on the glass.

3 Carefully press the painted fabric onto the painted glass, starting from one side; place a layer of newspaper over it and lightly rub over the entire surface. Remove the newspaper and carefully lift the fabric from the glass. Allow the paint to dry.

4 Draw the outlines of a lizard on the polystyrene tub. Heat the tip of the safety pin over a candle flame and carve out the motif with the pin. Stick a ball of Prestik to the back of the stamp to serve as a handle.

5 Apply paint directly onto the lizard stamp and carefully print it onto the painted cotton square. Make sure the entire motif is printed. Use a darker colour paint and stamp over a lighter colour. If the fabric has been painted in a dark colour, first stamp the lizard in white, leave to dry, then paint the lizard in the desired colour over the white print.

6 Leave the paint to dry completely; iron the cotton square to fix the paint.

7 Repeat these steps with the other cotton squares but use variations on the same theme, and different colour combinations, for an interesting collection of cushions.

8 Complete the cushion covers with any matching plain cotton for the back panels and finish off the edges with brightly coloured cord or piping. Zippers in the covers will make it easier to keep them clean.

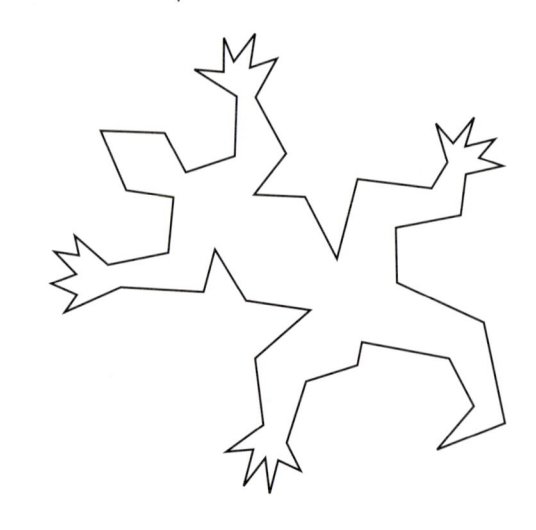

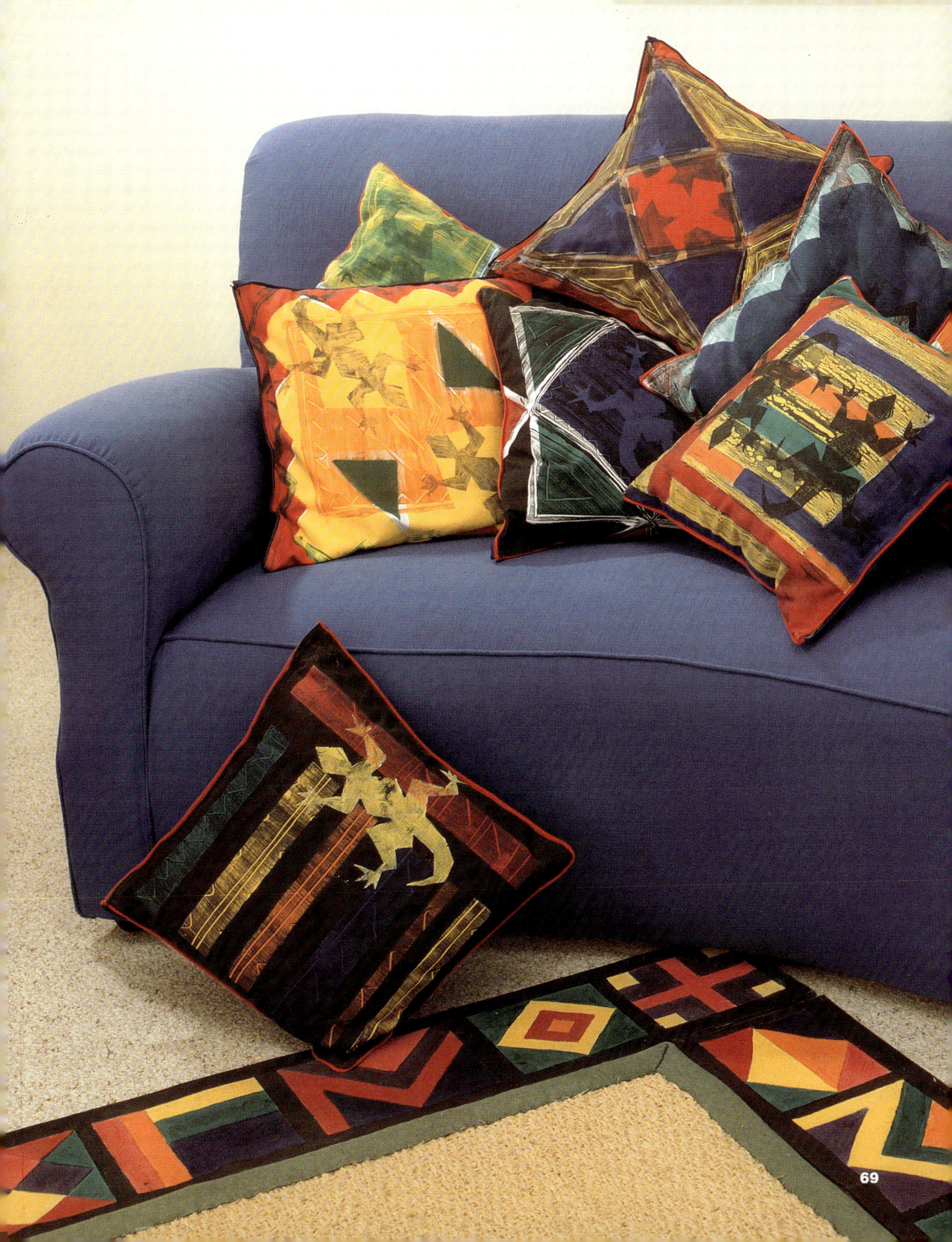

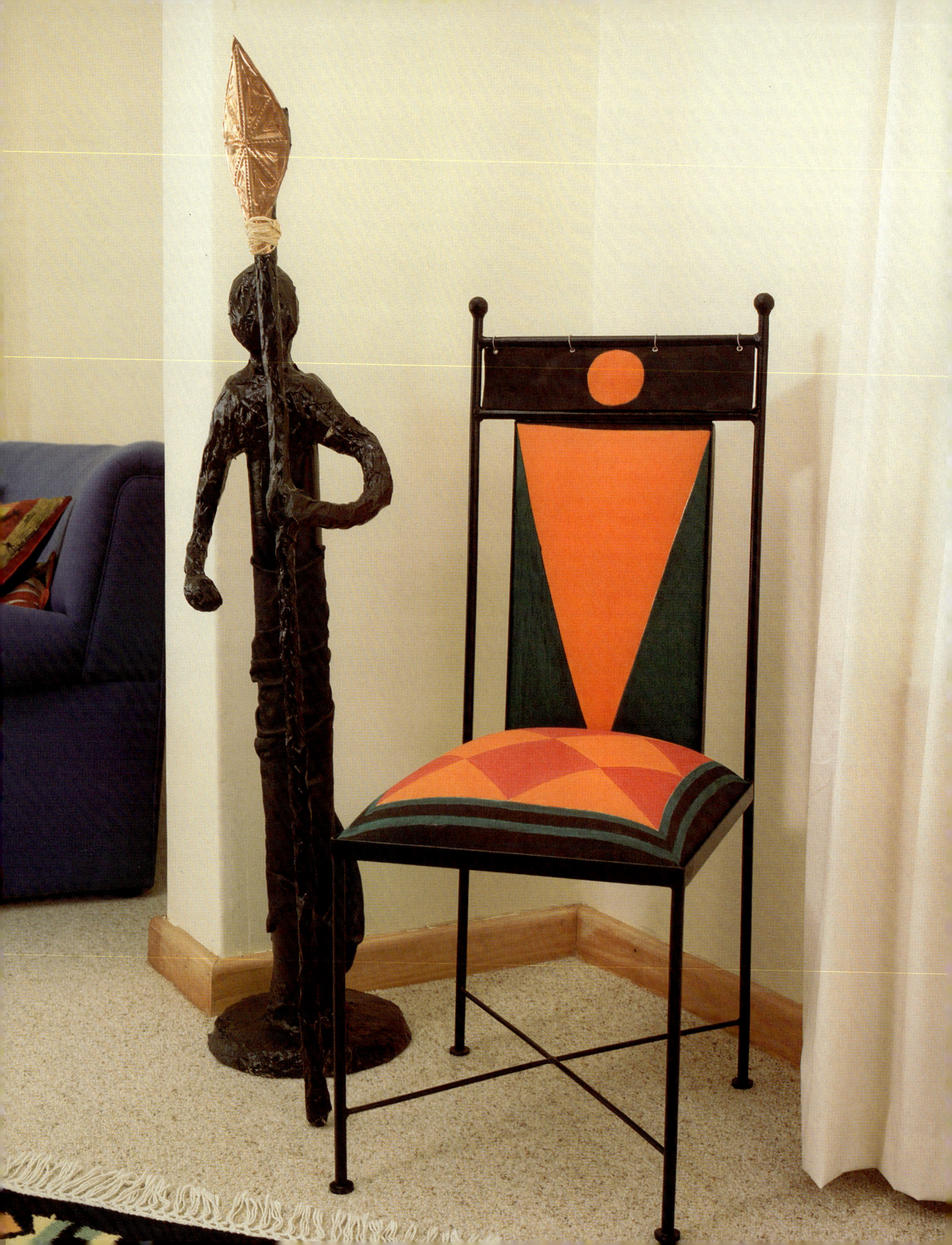

FABRIC PAINT

Chairs in Pairs

Although the wrought-iron frames will probably last a life-time, the seats of our diningroom chairs were faded and worn: it was time to give them a new lease of life with fresh, hand-painted fabric. I chose simple designs from the border pattern of a rug so that the entire family could help with the painting. To simplify matters, I divided the fabric squares into pairs before we started.

The chairs have an ornate design around the top of the backrests. I've never liked this so the cover and paint operation was the ideal opportunity to conceal this part of each chair under a cloth flap decorated to match the chair covers. Always use strong fabric for chair covers so that they do not wear out too soon.

1 Measure the seats and backrests of your chairs, adding 8 cm all around to allow for the upholstering, and cut fabric shapes to these sizes for each chair to be covered.

2 Frame the seat sections about 9 cm from the edge with strips of adhesive tape. Use more adhesive tape for an inner frame 1,5 cm from the outer frame. Paint the outer frame, as well as the lines between the strips of adhesive tape, using black fabric paint. Leave to dry and remove the adhesive tape.

3 On the backrest sections, use a ruler to draw a pencil line from the centre of the lower edge towards each top corner to form a large triangle. Paint these triangles on each pair of chair backs a different bright colour. Leave to dry and paint the background green.

4 Draw geometric designs on the seat sections of the chairs, changing the design for each pair of chairs. Use a ruler to ensure that your lines are straight. Paint the designs in colours that match the chair back parts. Use a fine brush to fill in sharp corners and a broad brush to cover larger surfaces. Allow the paint to dry thoroughly; iron to fix the paint.

5 Trim the corners of the painted fabric shapes; cover the seats and chair backs. Use a staple gun to secure the covers in position. (Paint your choice of design on the covers, but have the upholstery done professionally if you don't feel up to it.)

6 Optional: For each chair, decorate two rectangular strips cut according to measurement. Machine sew hems all around. Insert about four metal eyelets into the top edge of each strip, join the strips with wire ringlets and attach to the top of each backrest.

To fix the paint, iron the painted upholstery fabric before upholstering the chairs. It is a good idea to spray fabric protector on the surface so that you only need to wipe the chairs with a damp cloth when spillages occur.

You will need

strong white canvas; sharp scissors
(suitable for fabric);
adhesive tape; firm brushes
(thin and broad); paper towels;
pencil; ruler; fabric paint
(colours of your choice);
fabric protector;
eyelets & wire ringlets

PAINT – QUICK AND EASY

Two by Two Place-mats

The diningroom chairs decorated in pairs were so well received that I decided to use the same idea to make four place-mats, each with two place settings, for my square diningroom table that seats eight people. Adapt this project to suit the shape of your diningroom, kitchen or patio table. Make one place-mat for each side of the table, with place settings for two (or more) guests. The place-mats fit together in the corners like a puzzle. Or make a single round or oval place mat with six or eight place settings, all painted in bright colours.

You will need

strong plain fabric; scissors (suitable for fabric); dark lining fabric; cardboard; felt-tipped pen; craft knife; pencil; newspapers; brushes (medium and broad); paper towels; fabric paint; fabric protector

1. Cut four strips from the plain fabric to the following measurements: width 37 cm, length according to the sides of the table, plus 1,5 cm seam allowance on both sides. Cut corresponding strips from the lining fabric. Cut the short ends of each strip diagonally so that the strips will fit neatly in the corners. Always leave a 1,5 cm seam allowance.

2. Make a cardboard stencil to ensure that the design is identical on all the place mats. Cut a strip of cardboard the same size as half of the fabric strip. Arrange a plate, side-plate, wine glass and cutlery on the place mat. Trace the outlines of these items with a felt-tipped pen. Add 1 cm all round and cut out the shapes with a craft knife. Add other shapes if you wish.

3. Use this stencil and transfer the design to one half of a fabric strip with a pencil. Flip over the stencil and transfer the design to the other half of the fabric strip.

4. Place the fabric strip on a layer of newspapers and paint the design with fabric paint. Complete one colour at a time, cleaning your brush with water between colour applications. Leave to dry.

5. Line each decorated fabric strip with lining fabric: Place the two strips together, right sides facing; sew a 1 cm seam all around, leaving an opening for turning. Trim the seam and the corners and turn right side out. Neatly slipstitch to close the opening. Iron each table mat so the seams lie flat and to fix the paint. Spray fabric protector over the surface if you wish.

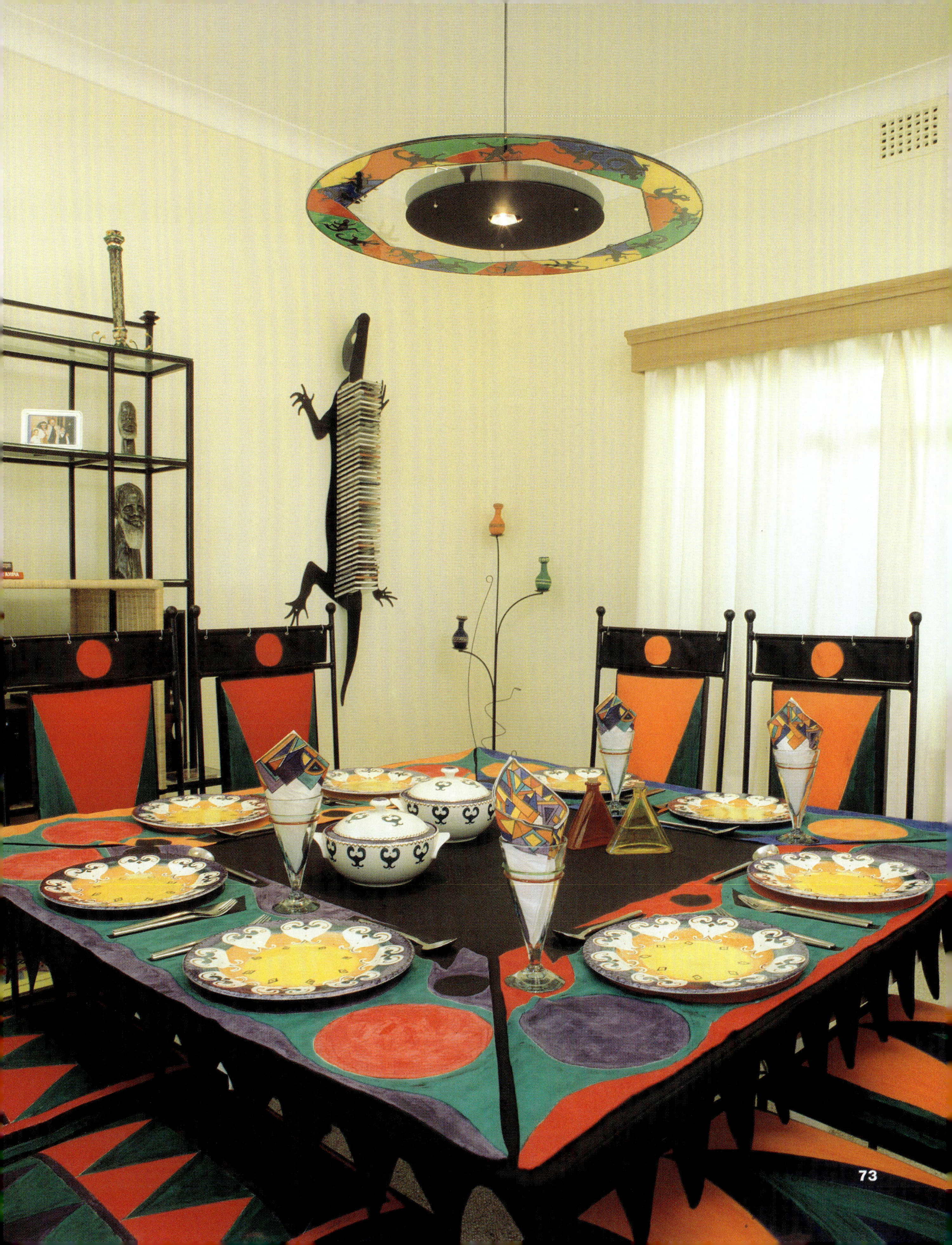

PAINT – QUICK AND EASY

Rugged Frame

The loose rug in the livingroom suddenly seemed so dull in the company of all the newly covered and painted furniture. Because it was still in good condition, I couldn't very well replace it with a new one. The neutral colour made it very versatile, so I wasn't keen on painting it at random. A colourful frame of canvas strips decorated with geometric designs was the obvious solution to give the rug new life. Fabric protector, such as Scotchguard, helps to keep it clean. This treatment can be repeated from time to time.

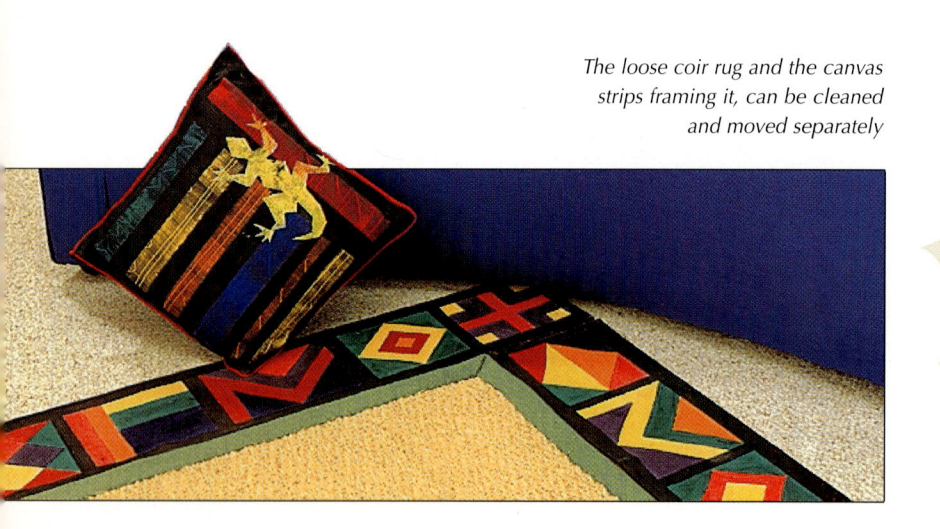

The loose coir rug and the canvas strips framing it, can be cleaned and moved separately

You will need

untreated canvas; strong contact adhesive; fabric paint; pencil; adhesive tape; scissors; brushes with hard bristles (thin and broad); paper towels; Velcro; fabric protector

This sketch shows how you glue both ends where two sides meet to the same Velcro strip. The burs of the Velcro strip are then pressed into the carpet covering the floor.

1 Cut the canvas into four strips, 55 cm wide and the same length as the sides of the rug plus 30 cm for the overlap. Fold in half lengthwise, sew the long seam, turn right side out and iron to lie flat. (Use a thick needle and special machine fittings for the thick canvas, or have the sewing done professionally. Alternatively, fold over lengthwise, make small folds along the edges and iron to lie flat; glue together with strong contact adhesive.)

2 With adhesive tape, paste down a frame along both sides of the canvas, with squares inside the frame. I divided the strips into squares and repeated simple geometric patterns in the squares. Apply black paint to the outer edges and between the squares, using a broad brush. Repeat with all the strips. Leave to dry thoroughly.

3 With a pencil, draw your design lightly in each square and paint in colours of your choice. Use a fine brush where necessary, completing one colour at a time. Clean the brush with water between colour applications and dab dry on paper towels. Allow the paint to dry completely.

4 Iron the decorated strips so that they will lie flat and to set the paint. Place the

FABRIC PAINT

strips in position around the rug, fold in the open ends to the inside and neatly line up the four strips at each corner. Slipstitch the openings or glue together the sides with strong contact adhesive.

5 If you intend using the rug frame as a loose rug on top of a wall-to-wall carpet, cut the burred part of the Velcro into four 25 cm lengths, apply glue to the smooth side and glue to the bottom of the edge where two decorated rug strips meet. This has two purposes: The strips are glued to each other and to the Velcro, and the burrs of the Velcro prevent the frame from shifting. The frame does not have to be attached to the rug and can be washed separately. The loose rug can also be cleaned on its own. If you are using the rug on a wooden floor or on tiles, cut underfelt according to the outside diameter of the rug frame and place the rug frame and rug on top.

6 Spray the rug frame with fabric protector. Repeat treatment whenever necessary.

The strong colours of the simple geometric motifs eliminate the need for finer detail on the rug frame. They complement the colours of the scatter cushions perfectly.

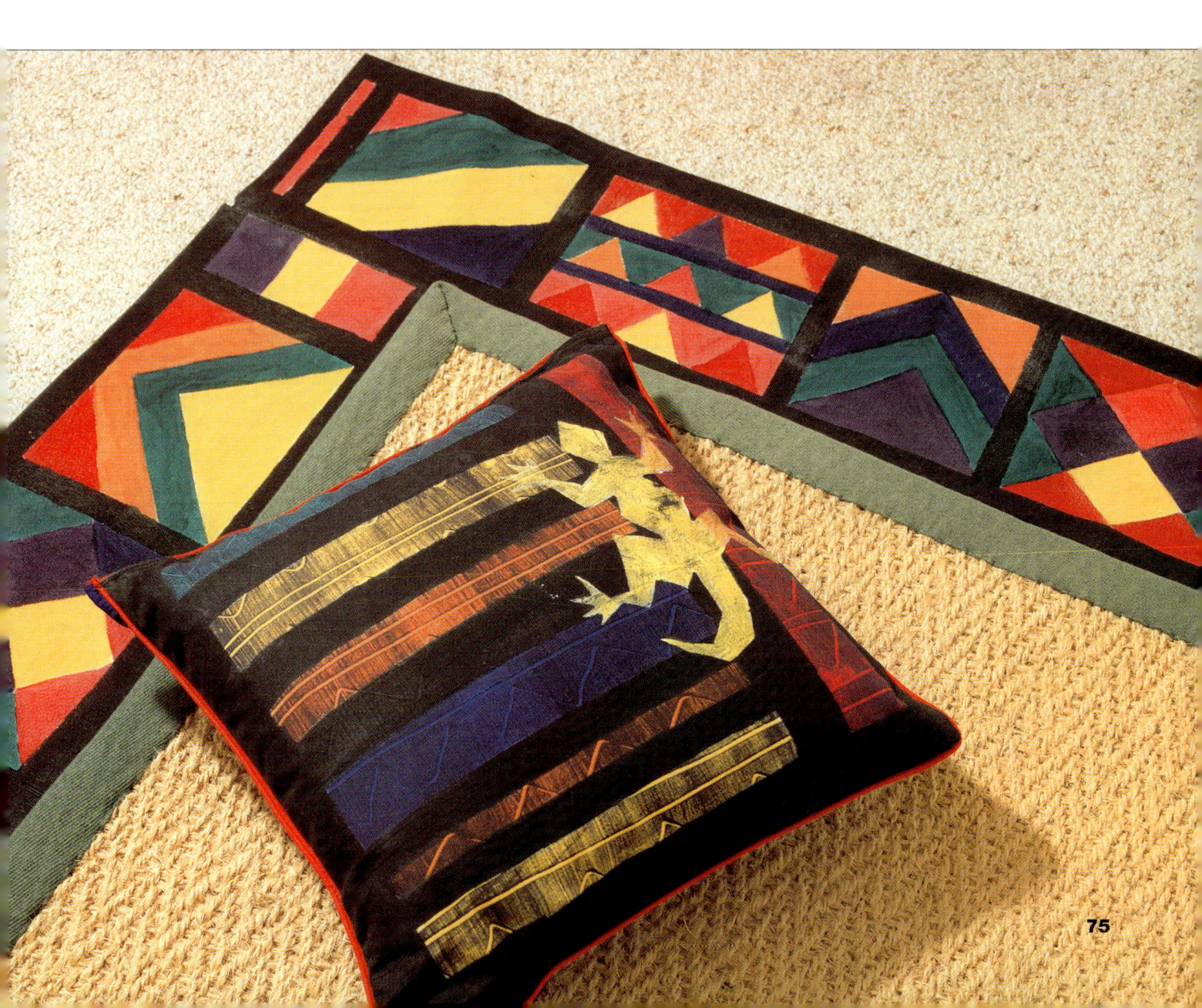

75

PAINT – QUICK AND EASY

Shining Example

I wanted to turn my children's artistic endeavours into something useful and decided to use their batik to make full-length lampshades. We had great fun cutting open old pillow-cases and playing with wax and paint. By using the short-cut batik method, we could finish the artwork in one day and use stamping as well. The children were surprised and proud when they saw the 'shining example' of their handiwork the very next day.

This is a lovely project for children as you can decide for yourselves to what extent you are involved.

The sketch above shows how the thin dowels fit into the holes drilled into the thicker dowels to form a frame.

1. Cut the paper into four rectangles measuring 26x17 cm. Let the children draw or trace four simple designs of their choice on the paper with a black felt-tipped pen. Themes such as marine life, or space scenes, or flowers or toys always work well.

2. Divide the cotton rectangle into four parts with seam allowances on both short sides leaving a clear strip and hem allowances on both long sides. Place the fabric over the paper designs and trace the design onto the fabric with a permanent felt-tipped pen.

3. Melt $^1/_3$ bees wax and $^2/_3$ paraffin wax; heat until very hot. Place the fabric on a thick layer of newspapers next to the stove. Dip a firm, thin brush in the wax; paint wax all along the lines of the first design. Lift the fabric every now and again so that it does not stick to the newspaper. Using the same brush, frame each design with a wax line.

4. Place the fabric on a clean wad of newspapers and apply fabric paint in different colours to all the open areas between the wax outlines. Leave to dry.

5. Stamp a matching motif all around the top and bottom edges. Use a ready-made stamp or make your own as described on page 66-67. Paint over the printed areas with liquid paint. Leave to dry.

6. Melt the wax again; with a sponge pinched in a laundry peg, cover the whole painted rectangle with a layer of wax.

7. Place the batik on a layer of clean newspapers with one sheet covering the batik. Iron with a hot iron to remove the wax. Replace the top and bottom layers of newspaper until all the wax has been absorbed.

8. Machine sew the two short sides of the batik rectangle (right sides facing) and turn the case right side out.

9. Using the dowels, make a lampshade frame for the batik cover as follows: Measure 4 cm from each end of the first thick-

er dowel and drill a hole straight through the dowel. Make sure the thinner dowels will fit into it. Repeat the process with the other three thicker dowels.

10 Turn the dowels with the holes you have drilled facing. Measure 2 cm from each end and drill another hole into each end of the dowels (*see* sketch left).

11 Make a frame by fitting the thin dowels into these holes. Fit the decorated lampshade over the frame.

12 Place the lampshade over the base of a bedside lamp. The batik motifs look really striking with light shining through.

You will need

white paper; black permanent felt-tipped pen; white cotton fabric; 85x45 cm (or old pillow slip) newspapers; paraffin wax; synthetic bees wax; firm brushes (thin and broad); paper towels; liquid fabric paint; fabric paint; stamp and stamping pad; sponge; laundry peg; iron; 4 dowels (1,5x45 cm); 8 dowels (0,7x20,5 cm)

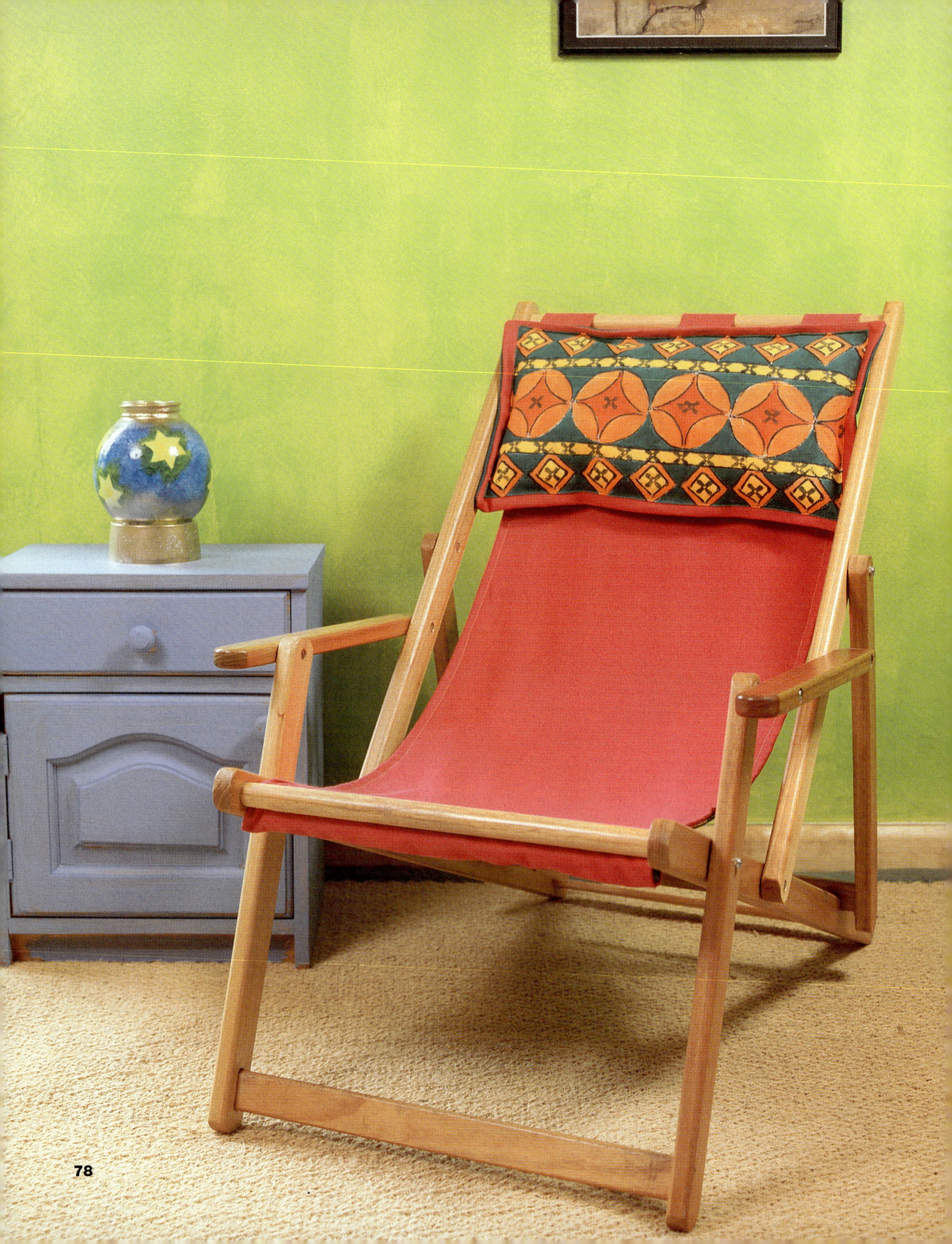

FABRIC PAINT

Beach Chair in the Bedroom

Convert an old beach chair to a comfortable and attractive armchair requires just a little patience and imagination. These two old canvas chairs were stored in the garage when the children recently moved into a new, larger bedroom with sufficient space for two armchairs. Before long the canvas chairs were upgraded and given armchair status. The stamped string motifs on the flip-over headrests looks striking against the plain background, and the technique and patterns can be repeated in other furnishings in the room.

1 Remove the old canvas from the chair, measure and cut the plain cotton fabric the same size plus 1 cm seam allowance and the necessary allowance at the top and bottom for a casing to insert the dowels.

2 Press a hem all around the cotton rectangle and machine sew to the long sides of the canvas. Make folds at the top and bottom ends and sew, retaining the dowel casings.

3 Make different stamps with cardboard and string, as well as a stamping pad, as described on pages 66-67.

4 Saturate the stamping pad with black fabric paint, press the string stamps into the paint (make sure the paint covers all the string parts) and stamp a repetitive pattern of string motifs onto the white cotton rectangle. Leave the paint to dry.

5 Carve a smaller stamp from an eraser or potato as described on pages 66-67. Stamp filler motifs between the string motifs and leave the paint to dry.

6 With a medium brush, apply fabric paint in colours of your choice to the areas between the stamped motifs; leave to dry.

7 Cut two rectangles, 54x30 cm, from the plain cotton fabric. Sew together, leaving an opening, and turn right side out. Press the seams and slipstitch the opening. Cut three strips, 17x7 cm, fold in half lengthwise, sew the long seam, turn right side out and press.

8 Fold and press a hem all around the painted rectangle. Pin it to the stitched casing, and position one end of each of the three plain fabric strips evenly spaced in the seam at the top. Machine sew, leaving an opening the size of your hand. Press.

9 Sew the other ends of the fabric strips to the seam of the top dowel casing so that the decorated part of the cushion cover is on the outside when flipped over the top dowel. Fill the cushion cover evenly with polyester filling. Slipstitch the opening.

10 Insert the wooden dowels through the casings and place the new chair cover back in its wooden frame. Flip the cushion over the top dowel to serve as a headrest. And ... relax!

Repeat the stamped motifs and colours used on the headrest elsewhere in the room to consolidate the theme.

You will need

per chair: 1x1,5 m plain cotton fabric; pins; 54x30 cm white cotton fabric (or old pillow-case); fabric paint; paper towels; firm brush (medium); stiff cardboard; soft string; contact adhesive; eraser or potato; craft knife; sponge (3 mm thick); Prestik; polyester filling

PAINT – QUICK AND EASY

Bedding in a Roll

My children pleaded for their own futons, passionately promising that their room would then be tidy forever. But in spite of all their promises, the duvets always looked untidy, especially on the low futons. It was up to me to find a solution and after some cutting and decorating, I came up with this cover for a bedding roll. Now the children keep their promise by rolling up their duvets every morning. The rectangular slipcase stitched to the cover is handy for storing pajamas, slippers and cuddly toys.

This project gave me the opportunity to repeat the string stamping technique which I used on the chairs. To roll up the whole works in the morning: at the head of the bed, tuck the decorated cover under the sheet. Tuck in the long sides of the duvet and the sheet so that the bedding will fit into the decorated cover; roll up the bedding, starting at the foot of the bed up to the head where the cover is tucked under the sheet. Roll up the cover with the bedding until the two Velcro strips meet. Press together the Velcro strips, pull tight the cord on either side and tie the ends. The bedding roll is not only practical, but also contributes to the colourful decoration of the room.

You will need

per bedding cover: strong plain fabric (107x82 cm); strong white fabric; Velcro; fabric paint; firm brush; paper towels; soft thin string; thin sponge; strong cardboard; contact adhesive; Prestik; thin elastic; thin cord

Making the bed will become an adventure with this colourful bedding roll cover – your children may even enjoy tidying their rooms (Moms are also allowed to dream!)

1 From the white fabric, cut two strips measuring 107x10 cm and one rectangle measuring 72x20 cm. Apply three different colours of fabric paint in bands to both long strips and leave to dry.

2 Machine sew one strip to each side of the plain fabric; press and sew a hem all around. Sew a casing in the outer edge of each painted strip for the cord to be threaded through. Cut a strip of Velcro of about 100 cm, pull apart the two sides and sew to the top and bottom edges of the plain fabric rectangle: one side on the outside and the other on the inside.

3 Cut a 72x20 cm rectangle from the strong white fabric and decorate by stamping with string motifs, filling in colours in the open areas to match the headrest of the canvas chair (as described on page 79), or use motifs and stamps of your own choice. Leave to dry, press a hem into all four sides and iron to flatten the hem and to fix the paint.

4 Stitch thin elastic to the inside of one long side, gathering it slightly.

5 Pin the decorated rectangle to the main part with the bottom edge 13 cm from the Velcro strip on the outside of the main panel, more or less in the middle. Machine sew the sides of the decorated rectangle to the main panel. Pin the bottom edge in the centre and fold a pleat at both ends so that the gathered top edge lies flat. Sew the bottom edge of the decorated rectangle to the main panel.

6 Thread cord through the casings in the sides. Roll up the bedding together with the cover as described above, press together the Velcro strips, tighten the cord and tie.

81

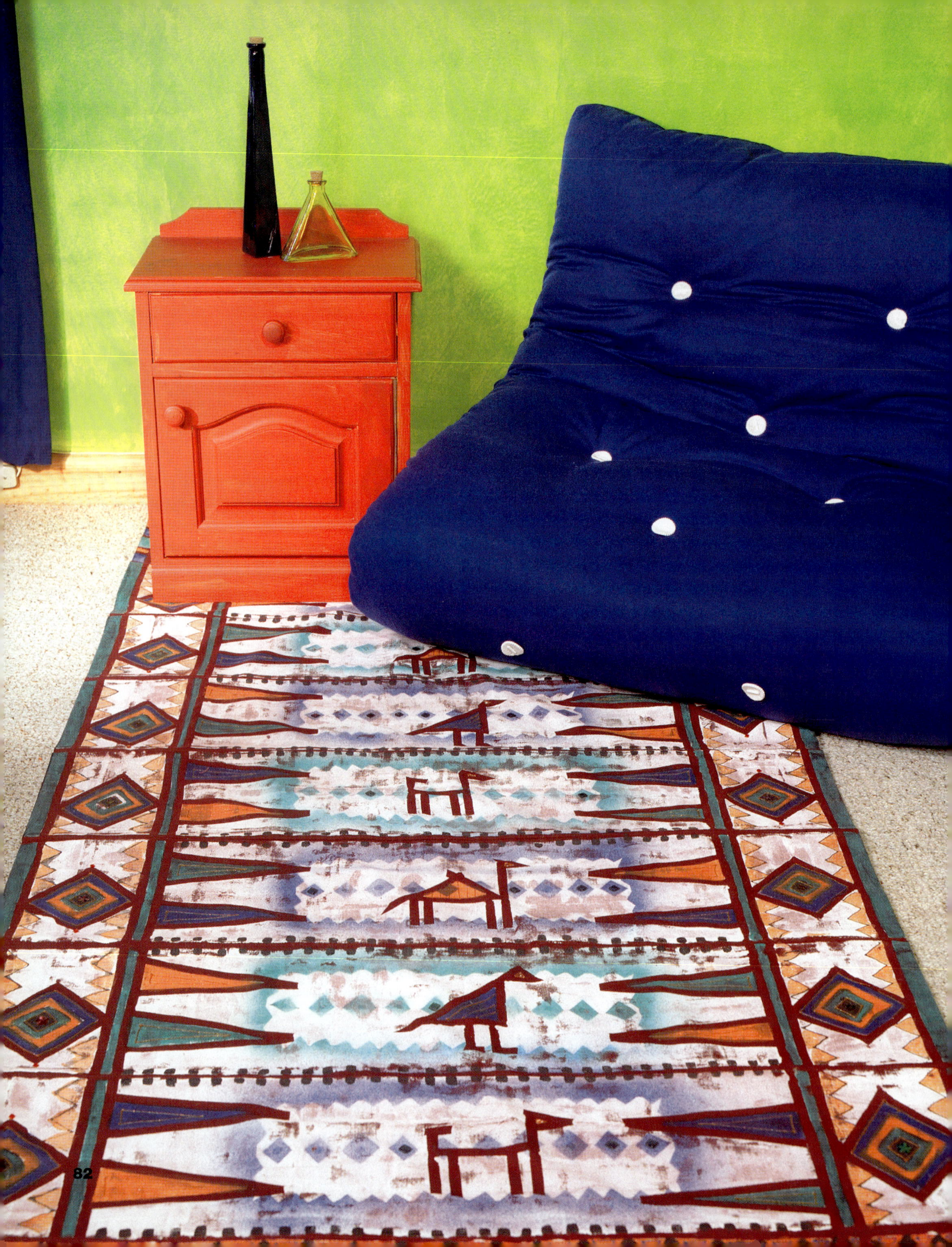

FABRIC PAINT

From Wall to Floor

My son's burgundy Roman blind was too small for the window of his new room, so we had to decide on its future. It was made of strong fabric and still in good condition. Besides, it was neatly lined and could do heavier duty than decorating a window. 'Why not turn the blind into a kelim?' I thought, and immediately began to work on it. Fabric paint has a transparent base and light colours would therefore not show up on the dark burgundy. I solved this problem by first masking several patterns with adhesive tape (the masked parts would remain burgundy). Then I applied white acrylic paint to the entire blind. Now I could decorate the rest of the kelim with fabric paint in any other colour.

If you do not have an old blind to begin with, buy strong canvas in a dark colour, line it with strong unbleached calico and follow the rest of the instructions.

Always try to look beyond the obvious function of items such as blinds when they can no longer fulfil their original function. In this case the kelim is even more effective as a kelim than it ever was as a blind!

1. Remove the dowels, cord and rings and place the blind/canvas rectangle on a layer of newspaper. Lay down strips of adhesive tape in geometrical patterns and blocks around the edge, and masking out simple animal motifs down the centre (*see* photograph).

2. Pour white acrylic paint into the paint tray and apply paint evenly over the entire kelim with the paint roller. Using a roller results in an uneven paint finish which suits a kelim. Leave until completely dry.

3. Using fabric paint in different colours, add further geometrical patterns or whatever you fancy in the blocks you formed with adhesive tape. Leave to dry.

4. Remove all the strips of adhesive tape and fill in finer detail with dark-coloured fabric paint on the burgundy parts. Leave to dry.

5. If you wish, finish off with tassels or thick cord and place the kelim on underfelt cut according to size.

6. Apply at least one coat of fabric protector.

You will need

unused blind or strong canvas rectangle, lined; newspaper adhesive tape; scissors; white acrylic paint; paint roller and tray; paint brushes; fabric paint; paper towels; fabric protector; underfelt tassels and cord (optional)

PAINT – QUICK AND EASY

Glowing Bouquet

An element of surprise is my main motivation when it comes to decorating a room. A spare room is often neglected when a home is being renovated, so this one required special motivation. Inspiration came when I decided to combine batik motifs and black fabric to create a 'glow-in-the-dark' effect. Once the batik motifs were in place they looked so pretty it seemed a shame to hide them away when the blind is pulled up during the day. Hence a window blind that opens when you let it down, and closes when you pull it up. The result is a glowing bouquet of flowers displayed on the wall all day. A frame in the same black fabric finishes off the picture while concealing the cord and hooks of the blind. I will briefly describe how the blind is assembled but if you don't feel up to the mechanical part of the project, ask a professional to handle it.

You will need

strong black fabric; thin white cotton fabric; pencil; bees wax; paraffin wax; paper towels; firm paint brushes; liquid fabric paint (such as dye or silk paint); old sponge; laundry peg; iron; newspaper; scissors; fabric glue; black appliqué glue; gold and black fabric paint; orange cotton fabric; 2 long wooden poles; 2 wooden brackets; nylon cord; 4 screw eyelets; 2 rings; 1 single pulley; 1 double pulley; Velcro; 2 short wooden battens

The 'frame' of black cotton fabric is an unusual finishing touch and makes for a blind as pretty as a picture during the day and at night. It is attached to the pelmet with Velcro strips.

1 Measure the window and add 14 cm to the width and 16 cm to the length. To these measurements, cut a piece of black fabric for the blind. Plan the size of your design so that it fits neatly into the blind area.

2 On the white fabric, draw simple flower and leaf motifs ranging in size from 18 to 25 cm. Apply wax and liquid fabric paint to these motifs, using the short-cut batik method described on page 67. Do not crack the final wax layer before ironing the batik. Once all the wax has been absorbed, cut out all the motifs, adding about 1 cm around the outer edges.

3 Following your design, arrange the batik motifs, face up, on the right side of the fabric cut for the blind. Draw a light pencil line around each motif. Remove the motifs and apply appliqué glue in a matching colour 1 cm inside the pencil lines. Leave the glue to dry completely.

4 Cut out the motif shapes along the inside of the appliqué glue lines on the blind panel. The appliqué glue prevents the fabric from fraying, so don't cut through the lines. On the wrong side of the blind panel, apply glue around the edge of a cut-out shape; paste the corresponding batik motif into the cut-out shape, face down. Repeat with all the motifs and allow the glue to dry thoroughly. Sew the motifs to the blind if you prefer.

5 With gold fabric paint, paint flower stems onto the right side of the blind panel and leave to dry.

6 Draw an oblong flower trough on the orange fabric. Apply appliqué glue along the outline of the flower trough and leave to dry. Cut out the oblong shape along the outside of the glue lines, taking care not to cut through the glue. Draw a zigzag pattern on the flower trough and paint it black with fabric paint. Complete your design by glueing the decorated orange flower trough onto the blind panel, covering the lower ends of the painted flower stems.

FABRIC PAINT

7 Machine hem the sides and sew casings in the top and bottom of the blind. Insert the wooden poles in the casings; the top one should extend about 5 cm on either side. The pole in the top serves to position the blind; the pole in bottom weighs it down to hang neatly.

8 Fit the brackets to the wall on either side of the window above the window-sill; rest the top blind pole on them. Screw eyelets into both ends of the pole where they extend beyond the blind and tie one end of the nylon cord to the screw eyelet on the left side.

With a pulley mechanism that lets you let down the blind instead of pulling it up during the day, the blind remains decorative.

85

PAINT – QUICK AND EASY

This sketch shows that the pulley mechanism is really quite simple.

9. Attach the pulleys to the inside of the pelmet; the single pulley on the left at the top and the double pulley on the right at the top. Make sure that the pulleys line up exactly with the screw eyelets. Take the loose end of the nylon cord from the left screw eyelet straight up and thread it over the single pulley; now take it to the double pulley, threading it over the back wheel. Pull the cord down to the screw eyelet on the right. Double it up without tying it anywhere; take the loose end back up to the double pulley, thread it over the front wheel from the outside and take it back down to the screw eyelet on the right (*see* sketch on the left). Tie it at that point. Take the cord you have doubled-up on the right-hand side and pull the blind to the desired height. Make a firm knot in the doubled up cord at the point where it reaches the bracket to ensure that the blind will pull up to this height each time. Hook the cord over the bracket to keep the blind in this position.

FABRIC PAINT

10 Follow these steps to manipulate the lower end of the blind when the top is let down with the pulley system: Fit a screw eyelet to the bottom of the window-sill on either side of the blind. Sew a ring to the inside of the lower end of the blind, in line with each screw eyelet. Let down the blind and rest the top pole on the brackets fitted for this purpose. Fold in the lower end of the blind, taking it up so that the fold reaches just above floor level. Hold it in this position and measure the distance between the window-sill and the lower end; add 10 cm (for knots) and cut two pieces of cord to this measurement. Tie one end of each piece of cord to the ring on the blind and the other end to the eyelet under the window-sill so that the cord has no slack. When you let down the blind, its lower end will automatically fold in and up, and a large part of the design will remain visible.

11 Optional: 'Frame' the blind as follows: Cut three strips of black fabric (the same fabric as that used for the blind) according to the measurements of the window and the distance from the top of the pelmet to the floor. Decorate these strips with gold fabric paint motifs that match the batik motifs on the blind. Leave to dry. Machine sew hems right around, except in the lower ends of the side panels. Sew the side panels to the top panel. Sew Velcro positive to the upper edge on the right side of the top panel. Using strong contact adhesive, glue the Velcro negative to the inside of the pelmet, on the front. Allow the glue to dry and position the frame by pressing together the Velcro strips. Measure the length of the side panels and sew casings. Insert a short wooden batten into each casing to lend weight to the side panels so that the frame will hang neatly.

The batik flowers look most attractive with soft sunlight shining through from behind.

PAINT – QUICK AND EASY

Dream Jar on a Wall

Nowhere is it written that every bed should necessarily have a conventional headboard, or that a headboard requires a fixed structure. So why not make a decorative wall hanging to double as a headboard? In my previous house this jar of dreams decorated a blind on my window. It did not fit any window it in the new house, so it now takes pride of place above the double bed in the spare room. I bought sheeting in the same colours as the fabric paint design on the side panels, and made a bedcover echoing the design. Adjust the colour scheme and motifs according to your own taste.

You will need

orange cotton fabric (150x150 cm); two strips of white cotton fabric (150x30 cm); black cotton fabric (at least 3,5 m); unbleached calico (2 m); pins; broad black ribbon; curtain rod (2 m) with finials and hooks; copper rod (2 m) and matching hooks; pencil; fabric paint; large polystyrene container; safety pin; candle; stiff cardboard square (14 cm x 14 cm); scissors; white glue; Prestik; firm brush (medium); paper towels; stamping pad

With such a bright and colourful headboard you cannot but have techni-colour dreams!

1 Fold a sheet of newspaper in half lengthwise, draw one half of the jar motif against the fold (about 75x25 cm high) and cut it out. Fold open, place in the centre of the orange fabric square and lightly trace the outlines with a pencil. Paint the motif with black fabric paint and leave to dry.

2 Cut a 14 cm square from the base of a polystyrene container. Transfer the ethnic wall-painting design to the square; heat the sharp point of the safety pin over a candle flame and burn-cut the inner circle as well as the four inner triangles. Burn-cut the shallow lines into the polystyrene according to the detail of the design. To ensure a sturdy stamping surface, glue this polystyrene stamp onto the cardboard square with white glue and leave until completely dry. Press a ball of Prestik onto the back of the cardboard to serve as a handle.

3 Saturate the stamping pad with black fabric paint, dab the stamp onto the saturated pad a few times, making sure the paint adheres to every part of the polystyrene stamp. Stamp the motif repeatedly along the length of the two strips of white fabric. Leave the black paint to dry, then fill in the rest of the colours of your choice with a medium brush. Leave the paint to dry thoroughly.

4 Machine sew the decorated strips to the sides of the orange square. Cut three strips of black fabric, two measuring 150x20 and one measuring 190x20 cm; stitch these to the sides and lower end of the decorated panel, framing it. Line the framed panel with unbleached calico and iron to heat-set the the paint and so that it lies flat.

5 Sew a casing at the top of the panel and insert the copper rod through the casing. Fit hooks to the wall and hang the panel on the wall so that the lower end is in line with the mattress.

6 Cut a strip of black fabric, 200x70 cm, fold in half lengthwise (right sides facing with opening at the top), pin eight equilateral triangles of 25 cm from side to side and machine sew accordingly (a band of 10 cm must remain at the top). Cut away the remaining fabric along the sewing lines, sew the side seams for the 10 cm band and cut notches in the corners. Turn the pointed strip right side out, neaten the corners and press.

FABRIC PAINT

7 Cut the ribbon into nine lengths of about 22 cm. Fold and press a narrow hem in to both sides of the the open edge of the pointed strip; fold the ribbon strips in half and pin the rough edges into the opening, making sure they are evenly spaced. Sew neatly, catching the ribbon loops in the seam at the same time.

8 Insert the curtain rod through the loops and rest the ends on brackets, in line with the top end of the decorated panel which you have already hung. Attach the finials to the ends of the curtain rod. An inexpensive wooden rod painted black (mat finish) will look as striking as a cast-iron rod.

The ethnic design of the side panels was the ideal motif for the cotton bed cover.

89

90

FABRIC PAINT

Jar-shaped Lamps

Fabric paint can be applied to several mediums other than fabric. Because paper also has an absorbent surface, it can be decorated most effectively by stamping with fabric paint. To extend the theme of the rest of the furnishings in the spare room to the bedside lamps, I stamped the same ethnic design on handmade paper squares using an eraser stamp and fabric paint. I wanted to repeat the jar motif painted on the head board of the bed, so when I couldn't find a suitable base I improvised with throw-outs from the kitchen and papier-mâché to make these jar-shaped lamp bases. A small side-plate, painted black and glued to the bottom of the base lends sufficient support so that the lamp does not topple over.

1 Draw your stamp motif on an eraser and cut out with a craft knife. Stamp the motif in a repetitive pattern along the top edge of each paper square. Leave until completely dry and fill in the rest of the colours with a fine brush. Leave to dry completely.

2 Roll the paper into a cone shape; in the corner of the stamped edge, carefully pierce two holes through all the layers of paper. Thread raffia through the two holes. Tie the raffia into a bow at the front.

3 For the base, cut a circle the size of the cardboard tube in the bottom and lid of the margarine tub; insert the tube to provide for the electric cord which has to be threaded through the centre of the base at a later stage.

4 Loosely roll strips of paper towel lengthwise; wrap them around the outside of the margarine tub for a more rounded shape; secure with adhesive tape. Build-up the desired jar shape around the cardboard tube. Wrap and paste pieces of paper towel around the top end of the roll. Wrap aluminium foil around the paper towel padding so that only the tube openings remain open. This holds the paper towel in position and serves as a basis for the papier-mâché.

5 In a mixing bowl, mix starch and cold water to a smooth paste; add boiling water as instructed on the packaging and leave to cool until the paste is comfortable to handle. In the meantime, tear strips of newspaper into pieces about the size of the palm of your hand.

6 Dip the pieces of newspaper into the starch one by one and paste all over the aluminium foil. Allow the edges of the pieces of newspaper to overlap, making sure they lie flat. Lay down at least two layers of newspaper strips; leave to dry thoroughly.

7 Spray or paint the lamp base and the side-plate black and leave to dry. Decorate with simple patterns with acrylic paint around the ball shape and the top edge of the base.

8 Place the paper cone in the lamp base. Attach the light bulb fitting to the electric cord, press firmly into the top of the lamp base and thread the other end of the cord through the cardboard tube and out at the bottom. Cut a groove at the bottom of the base for the cord to fit into; secure the cord in the groove with strong adhesive tape. Complete the lamp by fitting a wall plug and a light bulb.

You will need

2 sheets of cream handmade paper (45x45 cm); large eraser; craft knife; stamping pad; fabric paint; brushes; paper towels; raffia; empty round margarine tub; scissors; cardboard tube (like the one inside a roll of paper towels); adhesive or masking tape; aluminium foil; starch; newspaper; black enamel or spray paint; acrylic paint; clear varnish; electric cord and fittings for the lamp; old side-plate; strong contact adhesive

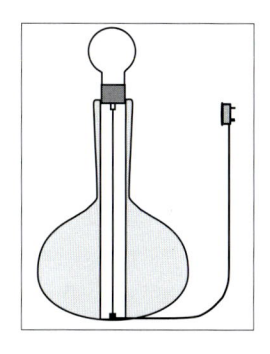

The sketch shows how the bulb and bulb fitting with the electric cord fit into the lamp base.

91

PAINT – QUICK AND EASY

King of Screens

Every house has is a room where a certain amount of chaos reigns – where needlecraft or school projects are tackled and games are played. There is usually a corner that occasionally becomes so untidy that it needs to be hidden from outside eyes. My rummage corner in the games room sometimes needs to be concealed in an attractive and practical way. For this purpose I found an old sheet which I decorated with a gigantic playing card to screen my rummage or work corner from the rest of the room. Now I am able to hide away when I want to be alone, but still be within earshot of the game playing.

Screw an eyelet into the wall and sew a ring to one corner of the screen so you can open the screen partly.

You will need

2 m white cotton fabric; 2 m plain cotton fabric; the king of a pack of playing cards; pencil; long ruler and tape measure; iron; black permanent felt-tipped pen; adhesive tape; firm brushes (thin and broad); fabric paint; large polystyrene container; candle; safety pin; Prestik; sponge, 3 mm thick sponge; stiff cardboard; cold glue; wooden pole; brackets; screw eyelet

1 Measure the opening into which the screen is to fit, add 30 cm to the length and width and cut the white and the plain cotton fabric to these measurements. Fold the white panel into squares. Press. Enlarge the card design and draw the corresponding number of squares on it. With a pencil, lightly draw the card shape on the white panel; use the block method (*see page 65*). Once you are satisfied with the design, trace the pencil lines with the black felt-tipped pen. Lay down two strips of adhesive tape 1 cm apart for the inner frame around the king; repeat around the outer edge of the 'card'.

2 Paint the frames between the strips of adhesive tape black. Leave to dry and remove the adhesive tape. Paint the rest of the design with fabric paint in colours that match those of the room. Use gold in the background and on the king's robe. Leave until completely dry and trace the outlines again with the felt-tipped pen if necessary to finish off the picture.

3 Draw the clover pattern to the desired size on the face of the polystyrene container. Cut out the shape with a safety pin heated over a candle flame and make a stamp as well as a stamping pad as described on pages 66-67).

4 Saturate the stamping pad with black fabric paint, dab the stamp in the paint, making sure that the paint adheres to the entire surface of the stamp (you can also apply paint directly to the stamp). Stamp rows of clovers onto the plain fabric panel and leave to dry.

5 Pin the two decorated panels together, right sides facing. Machine sew, but leave an opening. Turn the case right side out and slipstitch the opening. Iron it on both sides to heat-set the paint and to press the seam.

6 Fold over the top edge of the screen and sew a casing; insert the wooden pole through the casing. Fit the brackets in position on the wall and rest the pole on them. If you want to be able to fold away the screen partly instead of closing it completely, screw an eyelet into the wall at a suitable height and sew a ring in the opposite corner of the screen (see photograph left).

93

PAINT – QUICK AND EASY

Jacketed Chair

At some stage or another most of us have an old chair or sofa that needs re-upholstering, but we keep postponing it because of the cost involved. For me the solution was to make a loose cover for a desk chair, decorated with fabric paint in vivid colours to brighten up my work space. The shape of chairs differs and each chair will require an individual approach, especially if you are making a loose cover which you can remove to wash. The crux of the matter is that it can be done and that you can have the pleasure of turning it into a thing of beauty with fabric paint at the same time.

The sketch shows how far the cover reaches down behind the backrest and folds under the seat.

You will need

strong white canvas; scissors; pins; selfadhesive plastic; adhesive tape; firm brushes; fabric paint; paper towels; piping in matching colour; thin elastic; thin cord; fabric protector

1. Measure the width of the chair, then measure the length from under the seat (from the point where the cover will overlap); around the front edge, over the seat and back rest, over the top edge and down the back to the bottom of the back rest. Add 10 cm all round and cut a long strip of white canvas to according to these measurements.

2. Drape the canvas over the chair, exactly following its shape, and pin the sides neatly where possible. Neatly pin the top of the back rest, exactly following its shape; fold a hem where the sides cannot be pinned, for example at the arm rests. Carefully remove the cover from the chair, keeping the pins in position. Trim the excess fabric 2 cm from the pins. There should now be three panels. Remove the pins and place the longest panel, right side up, on a work surface.

3. Draw a poppy on self-adhesive plastic, cut it out and centre it in the top half of the long panel. With a broad brush, paint the whole top half purple. Work carefully around the edges of the masked poppy. Mix a small amount of purple and white fabric paint and apply with large brush strokes over the dark purple area. With the back of a brush, make a repetitive pattern in the wet paint for texture. Peel off the adhesive plastic motif, stick it on wax paper and wipe clean with a wet cloth so that you can use it again.

4. When the purple paint is dry, paint the white areas, as well as the bottom half of this panel, with orange fabric paint. Leave to dry. Fill in detail on the poppy with a fine brush and black paint.

5. With adhesive tape, mask 3 cm wide strips 3 cm apart on the orange half. Apply purple fabric paint. If you wish, repeat the scribbling process for texture. Leave to dry and remove the adhesive tape.

6. Paint the overlapping panel of the seat with orange fabric paint. Centre the poppy motif on the overlapping panel of the back rest; paint this panel with orange fabric paint and leave to dry. Fill in the masked area with purple paint, leave to dry and add detail with black paint (use a fine brush).

7. Drape the main panel, face down, over the chair; neatly pin it to the overlapping panels, right sides together, as in step 2. Mark the position of the arm rests. Remove, baste the seam with piping in position and machine

FABRIC PAINT

sew the seams. Sew neat hems, at the same time securing the piping, where the arm rests fit in. Stitch thin elastic into both overlapping edges so that the cover fits snugly. Turn right side out. Iron both sides to heat-set the paint.

8 Cover the chair with the completed cover. If required, attach cord on side of the cover where the seat and the backrest meet and tie to prevent the cover from shifting. Apply fabric protector.

Adjust the shape of your chair cover according to the shape of your chair, and decorate to match the theme of the room where it is used.

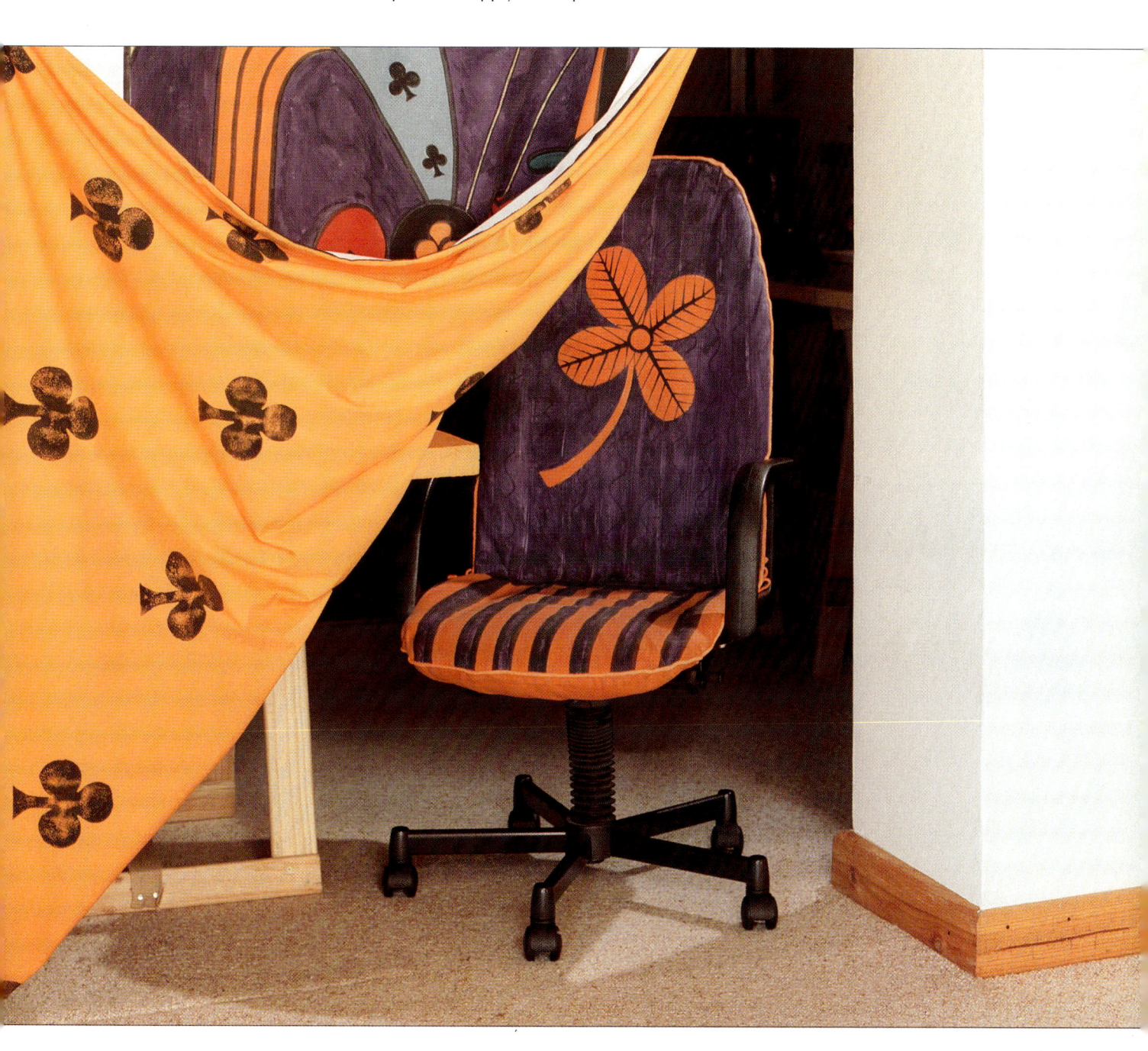

96

FABRIC PAINT

Jolly Jokers

Room dividers have many functions and can take on many forms. Our playroom is a jolly room where all sorts of activities take place. For this reason we chose a divider consisting of flags hanging from the ceiling at an angle and slightly overlapping, but free at the bottom. This means that games and equipment can easily be stored away behind it and as easily be retrieved. These flags can serve as a divider in any children's room or playroom or even serve to screen off a private play area or storage area in a classroom. When there is a slight breeze, the Jokers jiggle and dance, inviting everybody to join in the fun.

1. Enlarge the jokers in a pack of playing cards and draw four Jokers in different positions on rectangular sheets of paper. Divide the rectangles into squares. Fold and press the four white fabric rectangles into the same number of squares; transfer the designs onto the fabric with a soft pencil, using the block method. Trace the pencil lines with the black felt-tipped pen and complete the designs with fabric paint. Leave to dry.

2. Apply appliqué glue along the outline of each Joker, leave to dry and cut out just outside the glue lines (the appliqué glue prevents the edges from fraying).

3. Put together two green fabric rectangles, right sides facing; sew, leaving an opening. Turn right side out and press. Sew a casing at the top edge of each rectangle for the rods.

4. With gold fabric paint, paint a playing card motif at the bottom of each green rectangle, as well as the word JOKER at the top or on the side. Leave to dry. Frame each rectangle by laying down two strips of adhesive tape, paint gold and leave to dry.

5. Glue or machine sew the Joker figures to the green rectangles. Leave to dry if glued and insert the rods through the casings, extending slightly on either side.

6. Drill holes into both ends of the rods and fit screw eyelets. Screw eyelets into the ceiling where the flags are to hang. Make sure they are as far apart as the eyelets in the rods, and are positioned so that the flags will overlap slightly and hang at an angle.

7. Determine how high the flags must hang from the floor and cut eight lengths of chain or cord accordingly. Attach one end of each chain or cord to an eyelet on a rod and the other end to an eyelet in the ceiling.

Jolly multipurpose flags can function as a screen or room divider in almost any room. The playing card motifs used here suit the activities normally found in a playroom.

You will need
8 green and 4 white fabric rectangles (185x75 cm); fabric paint; firm brushes; adhesive tape; paper towels; permanent felt-tipped pen; black appliqué glue; pointed scissors; fabric glue; soft pencil; iron; white paper; metal or wooden rods (75 cm); 16 screw eyelet; thin chain or cord

PAINT – QUICK AND EASY

Say it with Flowers

Mother's Day and flowers go hand in hand and since my mother-in-law is always busy in the garden, a flower that would last a long time was the ideal gift for her. I chose the daisies because they are her favourite flowers. If you have enough time and patience, you can create a whole flower garden for your sunroom. Use flowers with simple shapes, such as sunflowers, poppies, tulips, and so on, with similar tartan squares as a background. Repeat the tartan effect on blinds, curtains, lamp shades, tablecloths, or whatever inspires you.

You will need

strong white cotton fabric;
plain cotton fabric; adhesive tape;
paint brushes; fabric paint;
paper towels; green appliqué glue;
scissors; polyester filling

White fabric paint motifs painted on white cotton fabric add texture and interest when further layers of paint in different colours are applied over the white-on-white motifs. The simple flower motifs painted in white before the rest of the design is completed, add a special touch to the cushion.

1 Cut a 42 cm square from the white cotton fabric. Lay down a frame of adhesive tape 3 cm from the edge, paying attention to neat corners. Lay down more adhesive tape forming an inner square 3 cm away. With a fine brush, paint small white flowers in the inner square and leave until completely dry.

2 Paste parallel strips of adhesive tape over the white flowers in the entire inner square. Paint between the strips with blue fabric paint and leave to dry. Remove the adhesive tape, paint the open strips green and leave to dry. The white flower shapes are a subtle colour under the blue and green fabric paint.

3 Stick adhesive tape cross-ways over the painted strips; paint blue in-between. Leave to dry and peel off the adhesive tape.

4 Paint the band between the taped frames blue and the outer edge yellow. With the broad brush, paint green over the wet yellow paint. Draw small flower motifs in the paint with a knitting needle or the back of the brush so that the yellow paint shows through.

5 Remove the adhesive tape frames. Paint the inner white frame yellow, apply blue paint over and scratch out a pattern of thick and thin bands in the wet paint with the back of a thick brush or knitting needle. Leave the outer frame white.

6 Cut two 20 cm circles from the white cotton fabric and draw simple daisy petals on it. Apply white paint to the leaves and green to the inner circle of one flower; scratch a pattern in the wet paint and leave to dry. Apply green appliqué glue evenly to all the

98

FABRIC PAINT

outlines as well as around the green inner circle of one of the flowers. Leave to dry and cut out both flower motifs just outside the appliqué glue lines.

7 Place the flower motifs with the decorated inner circle on top of the other; sew them to the square leaving the petals free.

8 Cut a square of 42 cm from the plain cotton fabric, place it on the right side of the painted square, right side down, and sew the outer edge, leaving an opening. Turn the case right side out, press to flatten the seam and stitch all along the lines of the inner square. Leave an opening again in line with the opening in the outer edge.

9 Stuff the inner square evenly with polyester filling and neatly slipstitch the openings. The first flower is ready to be planted in the sunroom!

Flower motifs are particularly suitable for this 'three-dimensional' appliqué. Sunflowers also work very well.

100

FABRIC PAINT

Fruity Blind

Giftwrap, magazines and children's colouring books are all excellent sources for designs to copy. To compose a design from individual items, first find a picture of each item, cut them out and then arrange them in different combinations, almost like a puzzle, until you find a combination that pleases the eye. Draw your design on a sheet of paper and enlarge on a photocopier. The block method is an easy way of transferring designs onto large surfaces. To speed up the process, fold the fabric into squares and press before transferring the design onto it. Use these methods to make a cheerful blind with fruit motifs for the kitchen.

1 Cut two rectangles from the sheet or cotton fabric according to the width of the window and the desired length of the blind, plus 5 cm all around for a seam allowance.

2 Draw squares over the paper design; fold the fabric rectangle into the same number of squares; press. Transfer the design square by square onto the fabric with a pencil.

3 Beat cake flour and water until slightly thicker than pancake batter and pour it into a bottle with a nozzle (an empty mustard or tomato sauce bottle works well). Trace all the design outlines with this starch mixture and leave to dry thoroughly. Sunlight will speed up the drying process.

4 Use fabric paint in different colours to paint the fruit and the background between the starch lines. Make sure the paint spreads evenly and allow to dry thoroughly.

5 Scratch off the hardened flour lines with a blunt knife. Use a cheese cutter if you have one, but be careful not to damage the fabric in the process.

6 Fold and stitch hems in both sides of both rectangles. Sew together the two rectangles at the top and bottom (right sides facing) and turn right side out. Press the seams and iron over the painted part to heat-set the paint.

7 Make casings for the dowels: sew a row of stitches 5 cm from the top and parallel with the top seam; repeat with another row of stitches 5 cm from the bottom and parallel with the bottom seam. Stitch another casing of width 5 cm in the centre, parallel with the top and the bottom.

8 Insert the wooden dowels into the three casings and complete the blind with rings and cord. Fit pulley wheels to facilitate rolling up the blind.

You will need

old sheet or white cotton fabric; pencil; cake flour; water; egg-beater; plastic bottle with nozzle; fabric paint; firm brushes; paper towels; blunt knife or cheese cutter; 3 thin wooden dowels; 9 rings; thin nylon cord; 3 hooks

The flower pot was painted with ordinary PVA and finished off with clear varnish to match the sunny colours of the blind. It now serves as a handy fruit bowl.

101

PAINT — QUICK AND EASY

Multipurpose Mats

I wanted to make place mats that could be cleaned with one wipe of a cloth and with this purpose in mind I bought imitation leather. I noticed that the backing of the imitation leather consists of a thin layer of fabric. This inspired me to experiment with fabric paint on the back of the imitation leather. My efforts resulted not in cheerful and colourful multipurpose mats: place mats, floor mats and even a mat for the patio table. Imitation leather with small factory faults is often sold in large quantities for next to nothing. Buy some and keep it until you are in the mood for painting.

You will need

imitation leather; pencil; scissors; white acrylic paint; paint roller; fabric paint; brushes; paper towels; varnish (Nova 17); turpentine

1. Plan you mat's size, shape and design and cut the imitation leather accordingly. I used a halved watermelon for the floor and matching watermelon slices for the table mats. With a paint roller, apply three layers of white acrylic paint to the fabric side. Allow to dry thoroughly between applications.

2. Draw the design on the white painted surface with a pencil and complete with fabric paint in different colours. Clean the brush between colour applications. Allow to dry thoroughly.

3. Apply four layers of varnish to protect the surface. Allow to dry thoroughly between layers and wait at least a day after the last application of varnish before using.

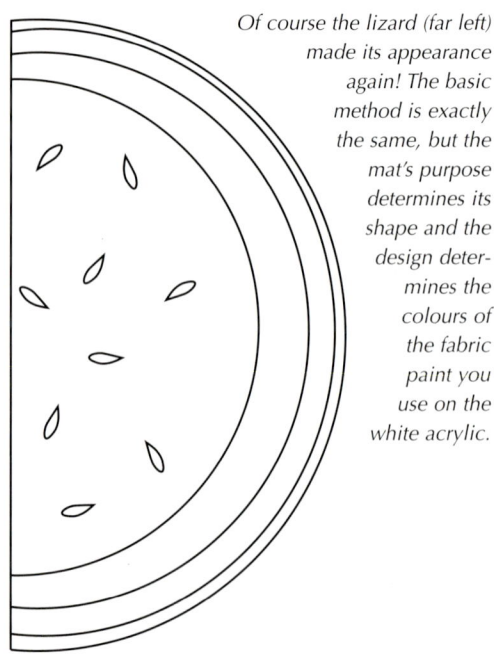

Of course the lizard (far left) made its appearance again! The basic method is exactly the same, but the mat's purpose determines its shape and the design determines the colours of the fabric paint you use on the white acrylic.

102

103

PAINT – QUICK AND EASY

FABRIC PAINT

Sunny Blind

With so many pots of paint left over from previous projects, it was only a matter of time before I combined glass painting and fabric painting in the same project. The obvious method for the fabric paint was batik, because the colours of both batik and glass paint are intensified beautifully when light shines through them from behind. This blind looks spectacular when the sun shines through, and with its light colours it lets in enough light so that it never has to be rolled up. For this reason I could make it to fit exactly into the window space.

You will need

thin cotton fabric; pencil; bees wax; paraffin wax; firm brushes; liquid fabric paint; paper towels; old sponge; laundry peg; newspaper; iron; metal eyelets and pliers; acetate or transparency; gold liquid-lead outliner; glass paint; skewer; safety pin; candle; strong orange or gold thread; needle; orange cord; 2 copper rods and brackets; thin wire; 43 cm wire ring; beads

1 Cut the cotton fabric according to the measurements of the window plus 10 cm all around for hem allowances. Draw a circle with a diameter of 42 cm in the centre of the fabric with a pencil. Draw wavy sunbeams from the circle towards the outer edges.

2 Place the fabric on a thick layer of newspaper. Melt ²/₃ paraffin wax with ¹/₃ bees wax in an old saucepan and use the short-cut batik method as described on page 67 to complete the design and the background. Keep your wax lines on the design as even as possible and work carefully when you crumple the wax-covered fabric to crack the wax.

3 Once all the wax has been removed from the batik design, cut out the circle in the centre and stitch hems right around.

4 From the acetate, cut a circle with a diameter of 43 cm. Place it over your glass painting design and trace the lines with gold liquid lead outliner. Leave to dry and fill in the different glass paint colours according to the basic method described on page 13. Leave the paint to dry thoroughly.

5 Heat the sharp point of the safety pin over a candle flame. Use it to make holes at regular intervals all around the edge of the decorated acetate circle. With strong thread, secure the circle to a wire ring, incorporating transparent beads. Place it in the circle opening in the batik, and secure it to the treated fabric. It can also be secured directly to the treated fabric, omitting the wire ring.

6 Insert metal eyelets into the top and bottom edges of the blind. Secure the top edge of the blind to a metal rod by neatly threading the cord through the eyelets and around the rod. Repeat with the bottom edge. Fit brackets in the required position in the window-opening and rest the rod secured to the top edge of the blind on these brackets.

The acetate circle can be secured directly to the treated fabric but by first securing it to a wire ring, you reinforce it. The beads are added simply as further decoration.

105

PAINT – QUICK AND EASY

Starry Drapes

Sometimes the ceiling in a room is too high or has unsightly stains which you want to conceal in a more interesting way than with a layer of paint. Have you ever considered bringing the moon and stars inside? Let the moon shine in the bathroom, guest toilet or nursery, and create your own matching galaxy. With short-cut batik and quick stamping you can achieve a spectacular effect without too much effort. Brighten up the mirror, tiles and bathroom mat with the same motifs using decorative stickers (see page 20) and printing.

You will need

thin white fabric; cardboard; strong blue canvas; blue appliqué glue; paraffin wax; bees wax; newspaper; firm brush; paper towels; liquid fabric paint; old sponge; laundry peg; iron; acetate or transparency; glass paint; pointed scissors; strong contact adhesive or fabric glue; silver fabric paint; stamping pad; eraser; craft knife; soft blue fabric; 3 wooden dowels; screw eyelets

1 First make the blind: Enlarge the moon motif to 54x40 cm and the star motif to 15 cm on newspaper and cut out. Place the motifs on the white fabric and trace them lightly with a pencil. Draw one moon and as many star motifs as you want.

2 Complete the motifs using the short-cut batik method on page 67. Do not crack the wax. When all the wax has been removed, cut out the motifs adding 1 cm all round.

3 Cut the blind from blue canvas according to the window measurements with seam allowances of 5 cm on either side and 10 cm in the length. Arrange the newspaper motifs on the canvas and trace lightly with a pencil. Draw as many stars as you made batik stars. Trace all the pencil lines with blue appliqué glue. Allow to dry completely and carefully cut out inside the glue lines.

4 Sew or glue the batik motifs into the corresponding openings. If you wish, add one or two stars cut from acetate and decorated with glass paint using the basic method. Use silver fabric paint to add finishing touches to the motifs on the front.

5 Carve a small star motif from the eraser and stamp silver stars in a repetitive pattern all over the blind. Allow the paint to dry.

6 Stitch narrow hems along the sides, as well as a wider casing at the top for inserting the wooden dowel.

7 Measure the length of the ceiling area you wish to cover, and cut a strip of soft blue fabric 50 cm longer than this measurement, and about 3 cm wider than the moon blind. Decorate with silver stars stamped in a repetitive pattern on it and leave to dry.

8 Hem the long sides and stitch a casing at one short end and another casing in the centre, for wooden dowels. Sew the other short end to the top edges of the moon blind. Insert a wooden dowel through the casing of the blind, one through each of the casings in the ceiling drape.

9 Rest the blind on screw eyelets fitted above the window. Screw eyelets into the ceiling where the centre and end dowels are to be secured. Rest centre and end dowels of the ceiling drapes on these eyelets. If the area you want to cover with the ceiling drape is very long, sew more casings and add more dowels between dowel holding the blind and the position of the end dowel.

FABRIC PAINT

PAINT — QUICK AND EASY

Stellar Window Treatment

You don't have to start a project from scratch if you wish to use stamping for decoration. Several months after I bought this simple, cream-coloured blind I decided to decorate it by using the star theme which was so successful in other projects. The neutral colours of the bathroom created a tranquil atmosphere which I did not want to spoil with bright colours. White stars on the blind and window drapes with a touch of gold were the answer. I made the star stamp myself, which did not cost me anything, so I did not mind spending some money on the sun stamp for the drapes. Since then I have used the same stamp for so many projects that it definitely qualifies as a handicraft 'investment'!

Using white fabric paint for the stamping results in a soft, subtle effect on the cream-coloured blind. This is complemented by the gold suns and stars on the window drapes.

1. Place the blind on a large, clean working surface. Wash the potato, cut it in half and draw a star on the flat side. Carve away the potato around the star shape with a craft knife. Dab the potato on paper towels to dry before you begin printing.

2. Saturate the stamping pad with white fabric paint, dab the potato in the paint on the pad until paint adheres to the whole star surface. Stamp stars in a repetitive pattern all over the blind.

3. Carve a smaller star shape out of the eraser, as explained above, and repeat step 2 with this stamp to fill the areas between the bigger stars. Leave the paint to dry thoroughly before you hang the blind again.

4. Make the drapes: Choose a soft fabric that hangs and drapes well, such as cheesecloth or voile, and cut it to the required length. Saturate the stamping pad with fabric paint: gold and other colours in a combination that suits the design. Dab the sun stamp in the paint on the stamping pad, making sure the paint adheres to the whole surface; print a repetitive pattern on the drape panel. Using gold fabric paint, fill the areas in-between with smaller suns and stars. Leave to dry thoroughly and iron to heat-set the paint. Press and sew neat hems in all the sides of the decorated drape panel.

5. Fit brackets above the window on either side of the blind. Secure the drape using a wooden rod slightly longer than the width of the blind. Hang one end of the panel along one side of the window; secure it to one end of the rod with thin string or elastic. Loosely drape the panel over the length of the rod and secure it to the other end, leaving the same length of fabric as was left hanging down the other side of the window. Rest on the brackets.

You will need

cream blind; large potato; eraser; craft knife; stamping pad; white fabric paint; soft white fabric; sun stamp; brush; paper towels; brackets; thin wooden rod; string or elastic

109

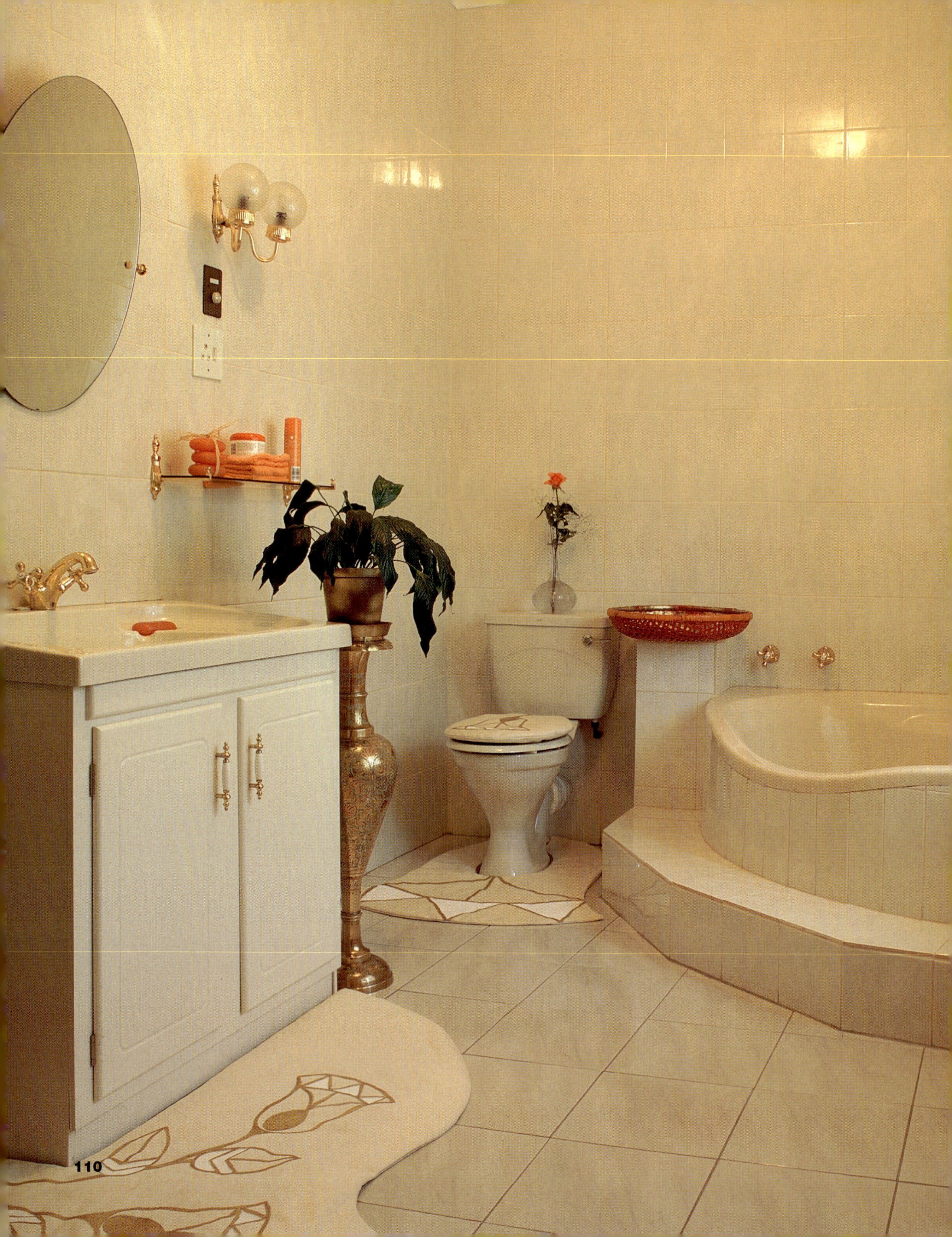

Fabulous Floors

The washbasin and shower in our en-suite bathroom were too far apart for one conventional bathroom mat, and two mats looked untidy. So out came my sewing machine and paint brushes. I made this running mat with its generous curves, as well as a matching toilet set, in no time. The result is quite sensational and I now feel like a movie star in a soap advertisement when I take my bath! Adjust the shape of your bathroom mats according to the shape and position of the shower, washbasin cupboards and toilet, and match the painted design with the theme of the rest of the bathroom or even the bedroom.

1 Draw patterns according to the shape of the toilet, washbasin cupboards and shower or other specific features of your bathroom on newspaper and cut out. If the shower and washbasin are very close together, join the two with one mat. Place the newspaper patterns in position on the bathroom floor to make sure everything fits before laying them out on the fabric.

2 Pin the newspaper patterns to the cream-coloured canvas, and cut out two of each, with a 1,5 cm seam allowance right around. Pin the newspaper patterns on thin sponge and cut out one of each.

3 With a soft pencil, lightly transfer the design you want to paint to the different parts of the mats. Use stencils, stamps and other suitable aids. For these mats I used a simple abstract floral pattern, and only white and gold fabric paint.

4 Fill in the colours one at a time and leave to dry thoroughly.

5 Place the right side of each decorated section on the right side its plain lining, with the corresponding sponge section underneath. Sew together the three parts, leaving an opening. Turn right side out with the sponge is on the inside. Slipstitch the opening with cream thread.

6 Make a cover for the toilet lid: Cut two fabric parts to fit the shape of the lid, adding a seam allowance. Decorate one section as desired to match the mats and leave to dry thoroughly. Place right sides together and stitch, leaving open the straight side at the back, as well as the last 10 cm along the sides. Turn right side out, fold and stitch hems in the open edges. Attach pieces of Velcro along the sides to secure the cover in position.

7 Iron all the painted parts to heat-set the paint and spray all the mats with Scotchguard fabric protector.

You will need

newspaper; pencil; strong cream-coloured canvas; scissors; white and gold fabric paint; paper towels; firm brushes; cardboard; eraser; craft knife; self-adhesive plastic; thin sponge; cream-coloured thread

By making your own bathroom mats, you can ensure that they are suitable for the lay-out of your bathroom.

PAINT – QUICK AND EASY

Sprayed Colour

With liquid fabric paint and an atomiser you have everything you need for quick and easy results. When you use this technique the paint remains on the surface of the fabric, so you can easily cover a metre with one bottle. And besides being simple and inexpensive, this technique is fun too! Place the thin tube in the paint and blow through the thicker tube. (Do not suck – unless you want to colour your teeth!) An automatic sucking action takes place where the two tubes are connected, a fine spray of paint comes out of the opening. Anything from a duvet cover, blind or tablecloth to cushion covers, place mats and T-shirts can be decorated with this technique. Combine this technique with others to achieve a different colour effect each time.

The sketch above shows how the atomiser is positioned with the thin tube in the paint and the thicker tube in your mouth. Use it to achieve an even spray effect.

1 Cut the cotton fabric according to the measurements required for your project.

2 **Tartan effect:** Lay strips of adhesive tape down the length of the fabric. Choose two colours, such as green and blue. With the atomiser, apply green paint to alternate bands between strips of adhesive tape. Clean the atomiser and apply blue paint to the remaining bands. Dab the adhesive strips with paper towels, peel them off and paste the ends to the edge of the table for the time being so that you can use them again. Lay down the same strips crosswise and repeat the process with the two colours. Dab the adhesive strips with paper towels and remove. Allow the fabric to dry thoroughly, iron to heat-set the paint and sew your article.

3 **Flowers:** Cut simple flower motifs in two sizes from self-adhesive plastic. Peel off the paper backing and stick the motifs on the fabric. Apply paint with the atomiser in the desired colour; dab the motifs with paper towels to dry and move them to the next area to be decorated. Clean the atomiser with running water between colour applications. Allow the paint to dry thoroughly. Iron over the paint to heat-set the paint and complete the article you are making.

4 **Leaves:** Collect any interesting leaves with a firm texture, arrange them on the fabric and secure them with Prestik if necessary. Apply the first colour with the atomiser; carefully remove the leaves from the fabric so that you don't get drops of paint in the wrong areas, and gently dab dry with paper towels. Arrange the leaves on the next section to be decorated and apply the next colour with the atomiser. Repeat until the entire piece of fabric is covered. Leave to dry and complete the article you are making.

5 **Roses:** Use the atomiser to apply spots of paint in two or three rose colours, such as yellow, pink and purple, to the fabric. Apply green paint around each colour spot in the same way. Use a fine brush, dip it into the first colour, for example yellow, and paint line detail on all the yellow colour spots to represent roses. Repeat with the other colours. Paint simple leaf lines in green around each rose. Use gold fabric paint for finer detail. Leave to dry thoroughly, iron the fabric and complete the article you wish to make.

FABRIC PAINT

More suggestions: there are endless possibilities ...

- This technique works very well combined with other fabric painting techniques. Use thick fabric paint for stamping free-hand painting or starch-masking designs in the foreground and use the atomiser to apply liquid fabric paint in matching colours to the background.

- Create a unique bedcover or duvet cover: Divide a large white sheet into squares with adhesive tape and combine the tartan pattern with two other masking patterns using the spray paint effect. Remove the strips of adhesive tape and stitch diagonal sew in a matching colour along all the white lines to achieve an interesting patchwork effect. Iron to heat-set the paint.

- Combine the spray paint effect (liquid fabric paint) and stamping (thick fabric paint) with similar leaves in autumn colours for a striking tablecloth and table napkins, or curtains, or even a long skirt.

You will need

white cotton fabric; newspaper; adhesive tape; self-adhesive plastic; leaves or paper doilies; scissors; Prestik; liquid fabric paint; atomiser; paper towels; fine brush

113

PAINT – QUICK AND EASY

Fishy Throw

When I wanted to use the stamp-printing method for a specific fish shape and could not find a suitable stamp, I used my children's modelling clay. The fabric paint stuck to the clay surprisingly well and the clay stamp was solid enough for continued use. In any home you will find at least one tired old towel or blanket. Transform them into a unique beach towel or picnic blanket by decorating a fabric rectangle with fish and shells and stitching it onto the one side.

Plasticine (modelling clay) is particularly suitable for making your own stamps because it is so easy to manipulate and can be pressed or rolled into any shape you want. To make any other patterns in the clay is child's play.

1 Cut a rectangle from the cotton fabric, 10 cm longer and 10 cm wider than the towel. Place it on a smooth work surface, such as a plank or table top and plan the design you intend to use for stamping.

2 Mould the modelling clay into simple shapes, for example a fish, a star fish and a clam shell. Flatten the stamping surface, and press a ball of clay to the back to serve as a handle. Scratch out detail on the flat surface with the skewer or press soft string into the clay for additional texture and then flatten the surface again on the plank or table.

3 Saturate the stamping pad with fabric paint in suitable colours. Dab the first stamp into it, making sure the paint adheres to the entire stamp surface. Stamp a repetitive pattern onto the fabric. Leave to dry thoroughly before using the next stamp.

4 Repeat the same process with the other clay stamps until you have completed the design to your satisfaction. Cut circles of various sizes from self-adhesive plastic and stick them here and there on the background to suggest air bubbles.

5 With the aid of the atomiser (*see* previous project), lightly spray blue liquid paint over the desired areas, as described on page 67. Clean the atomiser under running water and repeat with green liquid paint. Allow to dry and remove the paper circles.

6 Iron the decorated fabric to heat-set the paint. Fold and stitch hems in all sides of the decorated fabric, then sew to the towel or blanket and use.

You will need

white cotton or similar fabric; old towel or blanket; modelling clay (plasticine); skewer; stamping pad; brush; fabric paint; self-adhesive plastic; scissors; liquid fabric paint; atomiser; paper towels

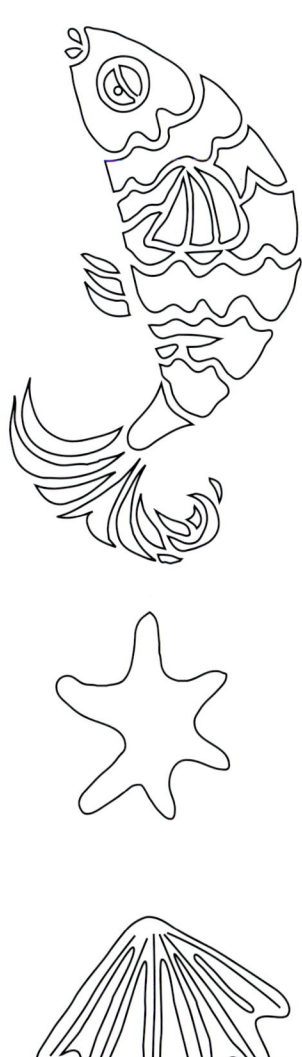

FABRIC PAINT

PAINT – QUICK AND EASY

FABRIC PAINT

Put your Stamp on it

Holidays needn't be a headache trying to keep your children and their friends occupied in a creative way. Keep them busy decorating a white T-shirt which they can wear themselves afterwards, or which they can give to a friend as a gift. Children have a short attention span but with the stamping technique you can be sure of quick results. It is also a very economical application – with 100 ml of fabric paint you can make more than 200 prints. If you want colour in the background as well, use the atomiser method and liquid fabric paint.

1 Wash the T-shirt beforehand to remove any starch. Fold a thick layer of newspaper and place it inside the T-shirt to separate the back and front parts. Make sure the newspaper has no creases or folds that will spoil the printing effect.

2 For the cat design: Lay down pieces of adhesive tape in the shape of a brick wall, apply liquid fabric paint with the atomiser and remove the tape. Cut out a moon from self-adhesive plastic (almost full circle), position above the the wall and apply another colour with the atomiser. Remove the moon shape.

3 Saturate the stamping pad with fabric paint in different colours as desired. Dab the cat stamp in the paint, making sure the paint adheres to entire stamp surface. Test it on a scrap of fabric, then stamp the cat as though it's sitting on the wall.

4 Carve a stamp of a cat's paw from an eraser or potato, apply black paint and stamp cats' paws all around the cat on the wall. Allow the paint to dry and iron the painted part to heat-set the paint.

5 For the guineafowl design: Saturate the stamping pad with fabric paint in your chosen colour combination. Dab the stamp in the paint and apply the stamp according to your design. The shadow effect is achieved by stamping a second time without dabbing the stamp in the paint again. Allow the paint to dry.

6 Secure palm leaves to the T-shirt with Prestik and use the atomiser to apply liquid fabric paint around them. For the blades of grass, apply fabric paint to a stamping pad, dab the edge of a thick piece of cardboard in the paint and stamp it on the design. Bend the cardboard and repeat. Crumple a piece of paper, dab it in the paint on the stamping pad and print it on the design to represent stones. Allow to dry thoroughly and iron the T-shirt to heat-fix the paint.

You will need

white T-shirt; newspaper; stamps and stamping pad; eraser; palm leaves; cardboard; brush; fabric paint; paper towels; liquid fabric paint; atomiser; adhesive tape; self-adhesive plastic

Something Extra

- Use eyes with moving pupils on the cat or sew beads and/or sequins to the guineafowl bodies for a smarter T-shirt.

- Use a black or dark T-shirt and decorate with stamping. Because white is not transparent, you can stamp your design in white If you want colour, paint the white printed motifs with different colours.

PAINT – QUICK AND EASY

Designer Denim

One day my husband remarked on my very faded jeans, the next day he couldn't find his denim shirt (it was too small for him anyway), and the following day I surprised him in a fetching outfit which had cost hardly more than an investment in time. Learn to look at your clothes with a creative eye before throwing them out. Jeans that have become shabby can be painted and worn with a matching denim shirt which you can 'borrow' from your husband. Once you have finished with it he won't recognise it anyway! You can transform simple, plain clothing items such as skirts with a pattern stamped around the hem into something new and fresh. Remember always to heat-set the paint by ironing the finished article as soon as the paint has dried.

1. Lay adhesive tape strips down the length of the front of the jeans and apply black fabric paint. Don't paint the waistband or the section above the pockets. Be careful where there are pleats and seams and always work from the adhesive tape strip towards the fabric to prevent the paint from seeping under the adhesive tape. Leave to dry.

2. Turn around the jeans and repeat the striped pattern on the back. Don't paint the pockets, the top triangular insert or the waistband. Leave to dry and apply paint to the sides, if necessary.

3. Using a craft knife, carve two square stamps, one slightly larger than the other, from the erasers. Saturate the stamping pad with black fabric paint, dab the small square stamp in the paint and stamp a repetitive pattern on the pockets. Alternate with the larger square. You can use any other geometrical shapes as well.

4. Decorate the shirt in the same way. Lay down strips of adhesive tape for the stripes to make sure that they are straight, and stamp further patterns with the square stamps.

5. Allow the paint to dry thoroughly and iron all the decorated parts with a hot iron to heat-set the paint.

You will need

jeans; denim shirt;
adhesive tape;
black fabric paint; s
firm brush; paper towels;
stamping pad;
2 erasers;
craft knife

More Ideas

- Use white instead of black paint for a striking effect on denim.

- Finish such a 'recycled' outfit with matching tackies decorated with the same design.

- Use liquid fabric paint instead of the ordinary thick fabric paint. Apply it randomly with an atomiser.

- Mask certain areas of the garment by cutting different shapes from self-adhesive plastic and sticking them on the fabric. Now apply paint around the shapes. Stamping in silver or white paint complements this masking technique beautifully.

119

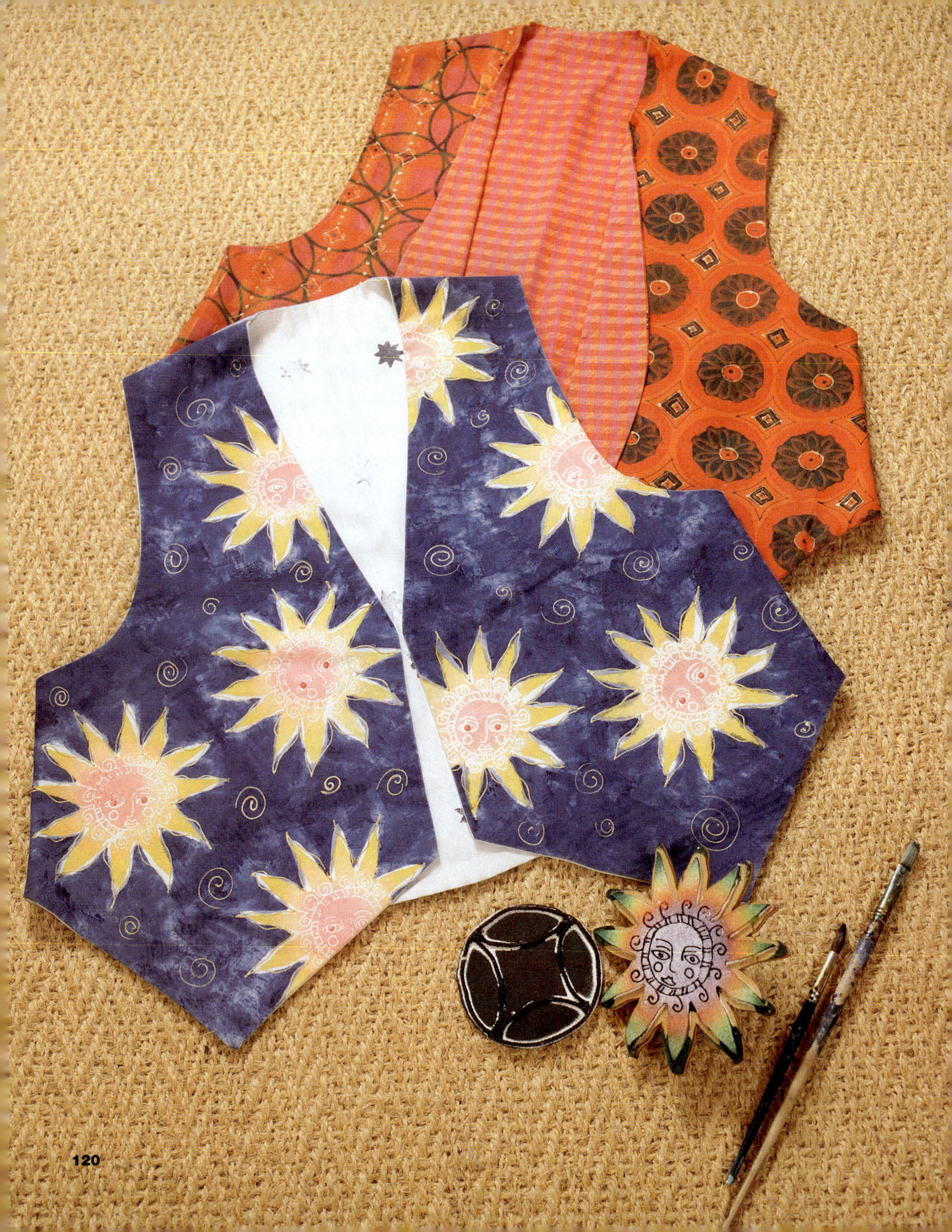

FABRIC PAINT

Reversible Waistcoats

A waistcoat finishes off any outfit and can even liven up a simple T-shirt. I traced the pattern of an old waistcoat onto white fabric and painted each panel in a different base colour. Armed with the round core of a roll of adhesive tape and an eraser, I stamped the design and finished off the painting with fabric paint outliner. The other waistcoat was decorated with my sun stamp and the background painted free-hand. Buy a waistcoat pattern or trace the pattern of an old waistcoat; then give your imagination free reign and decorate to your heart's content. Use contrasting colours such as pink, orange and red for an unusual end result. Any domestic object, such as a cork, potato or eraser can be used to stamp repetitive patterns on the fabric.

1 Cut out the different panels. Decorate only the right sides so that you don't become confused while you are up to your elbows in paint. Work with one panel at a time on a thick layer of newspaper.

2 For the waistcoat at the back: Decide on the basic colour(s), paint all the panels with a broad brush and allow to dry. Lay strips of adhesive down the lining panels; paint the open bands in-between with a darker colour than the background. Leave to dry, remove the adhesive tape, then lay down the strips of tape crosswise. Paint the bands in-between to achieve a check pattern. Allow to dry.

3 Decorate the outer panels as follows: Saturate part of the stamping pad with black fabric paint, press the core of the adhesive tape roll into the paint and stamp the shape as planned in a repetitive pattern onto the fabric. Stamp overlapping circles for an interesting effect. Use a different shape and a different colour to decorate the areas in-between. Complete the decoration by painting detail with a fine brush.

4 Paint round spots in a darker colour over the background colour (use the core of the adhesive tape as a stencil) and leave to dry. Paint smaller black spots in the centre of the larger spots. With the back of the paint brush, add line detail in the wet paint for interest and texture. Fill sections between the spots with stamping, for example with a cork. Finish off the painting and stamping with black fabric paint outliner where desired.

5 For the waistcoat in the front: Saturate the stamping pad with fabric paint in your chosen colours, dab the sun stamp in the wet stamping pad and stamp the motifs in a regular pattern all over the outer panels. Leave to dry. Paint the background free-hand in a contrasting colour and leave to dry. With gold liquid outliner, add finishing touches to the stamped motifs and add detail to the background as well. Leave to dry.

6 With gold fabric paint, stamp stars in two different sizes (use erasers) in a repetitive pattern on the lining panels. Leave to dry.

7 Iron all the decorated panels to heat-set the paint and sew the waistcoat according to the pattern instructions.

You will need

waistcoat pattern; white or cream cotton fabric; scissors; newspaper; adhesive tape; fabric paint; firm brushes; paper towels; stamping pad; soft string; stiff cardboard; cold glue; sun stamp or other stamp shapes (such as the core of an adhesive tape roll, eraser, cork); black or gold fabric paint outliner

The cloudy effect of the background on the front waistcoat has been achieved by randomly applying the colour in different directions.

121

PAINT – QUICK AND EASY

Stylish Toilet Set

Forget the ordinary toilet sets in the shops and make your own for your guest toilet. I used the fleur-de-lis motif again to match the candleholder and stickers which I decorated with glass paint, and stamped the same motif on the toilet set and magazine holder with a small stamp I carved out of an eraser. Then I carved the same motif out of a potato and stamped this on a strip of fabric, sewn to a small guest towel as a decorative border.

You will need

newspaper; felt-tipped pen; blue cotton fabric; thin sponge; scissors; eraser; craft knife; potato; stamping pad; white and blue fabric; Velcro or press studs; strip of white cotton fabric

Make a matching magazine holder: paint the inside and outside of a suitable box with white acrylic paint. Leave to dry and stamp-print fleur-de-lis motifs in blue fabric paint in a repeated pattern on the outside.

You can use any motif and carve a suitable stamp from an eraser to decorate a toilet set. Match the shape of the mat to the theme.

1 On a piece of newspaper, draw patterns for the toilet lid cover and a pointed toilet mat to match the pointed fleur-de-lis motif. Add 10 mm right around as a seam allowance and cut out. Pin to the blue fabric and cut two panels for each pattern part, as well as one sponge panel.

2 Carve a fleur-de-lis motif out of the eraser. Saturate the stamping pad with white fabric paint, dab the eraser stamp in the paint and stamp a repetitive pattern on the outside panels of the lid cover and mat. Leave to dry thoroughly before the next step.

3 Place the decorated mat panel on the mat lining panel, right sides facing, with a sponge panel on top. Sew right around, leaving an opening. Turn right side out, slipstitch the opening and press to make it lie flat and to heat-set the paint.

4 Sew the toilet lid cover, leaving the back and the last 10 cm of the side seams open. Stitch neat hems in the openings and attach Velcro or press studs to the sides to secure the cover in position.

5 Carve a larger fleur-de-lis stamp out of the potato. Saturate the stamping pad with blue fabric paint and stamp the motifs in a row on the strip of white cotton fabric. Allow the paint to dry; fold and press neat hems right around. Machine sew to the towel.

RENOVATING

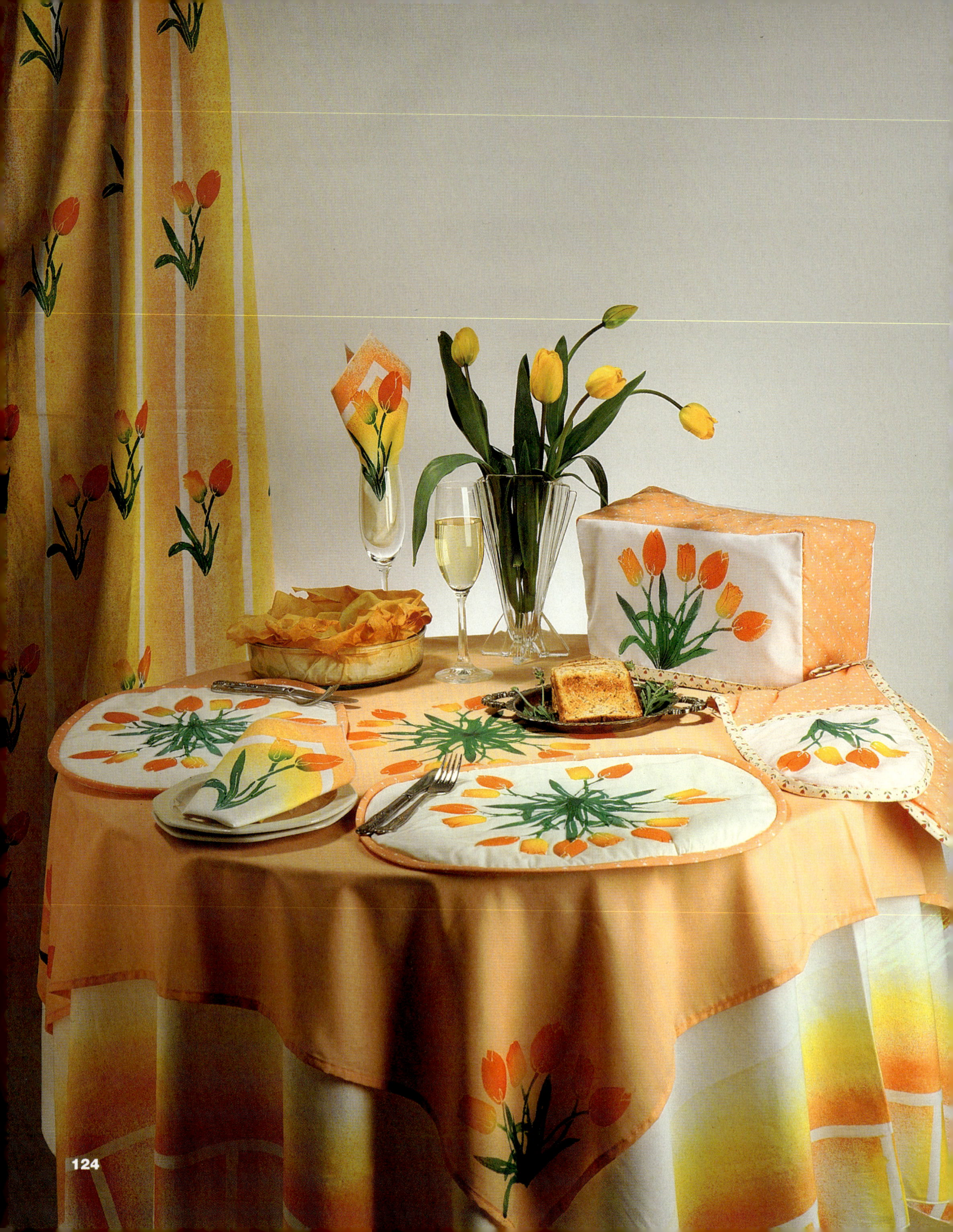

FABRIC PAINT

Tulips for Spring

Use tulips as a theme for a feast of colour in your kitchen – orange, yellow and green – just what you need to celebrate the end of winter. I used my ready-made tulip stamp to decorate my round tablecloth and table napkins. Once I got going nothing could stop me. Before long there were tulips on a throw, new place-mats, a tea cosy, curtains, and everything I could lay my hands on. These instructions are for making and decorating the tablecloth and table napkins, but I am sure the photograph will inspire you to tackle some of the other articles as well.

Fabric paint works equally well on paper napkins and tablecloths. Keep this in mind if you are planning to use an unusual theme for a special occasion.

1 Cut the cotton fabric according to the size of the tablecloth and napkins you want to make. If you are decorating a bought tablecloth, wash it before applying any paint to remove all the starch and iron out all the creases to prepare it for stamping.

2 Using a firm brush, apply fabric paint in the different colours to the appropriate parts of the stamp and press onto the stamping pad. Saturate the pad with paint following this pattern. Dab the stamp into the paint on the stamping pad, making sure the paint adheres to the whole stamp surface, but that there is no paint in the grooves as this will smudge and spoil the design. Stamp around the edges of the tablecloth and in the corners of the napkins according to your planned pattern. Leave to dry thoroughly.

3 Lay down adhesive tape around the edges of the tablecloth and napkins, then spray yellow liquid paint all around the edges with the atomiser. Rinse the atomiser under running water and repeat the process with orange liquid fabric paint for a fuller effect.

4 Iron all the decorated parts to heat-set the paint. Press and sew neat hems all around the rough edges of the tablecloth and napkins.

5 Take a good look at the shape and decoration of the other items on the photograph. Make one or all of them to match the tablecloth and napkins. Here are a few tips

- Plain-coloured piping in a colour that matches the fabric paint looks pretty around the place-mats and also makes it easier to finish them off.

- Use a work surface that is large enough for completely unfolding the cotton fabric for the curtains – this will help you to apply the colour spray evenly.

- Cut imitation leather to the desired size and shape for a floor mat (*see* page 102); paint with white acrylic paint, leave to dry and decorate with tulips and colour spray.

You will need

white cotton fabric or tablecloth and table napkins; scissors; stamp; fabric paint; stamping pad; paper towels; adhesive tape; newspaper; atomiser; liquid fabric paint

The dainty print pattern on the cotton fabric used for the toaster cover and potholder goes beautifully with the stamped tulips.

125

PAINT – QUICK AND EASY

Spotted Guineafowl

The guineafowl stamp used for this project is my favourite by far, mainly because the shadow printing adds so much dimension it looks as though a whole flock of guineafowl is traipsing across the veld. To complement the white flecked plumage, lay down round stickers all around edge of the cushion and tablecloth and spray with liquid fabric paint using an atomiser. When you peel off the stickers, the white spots place your guineafowl right in the spotlight!

These instructions are for the cushion only, but don't let that stop you from making a matching tablecloth, a lampshade, table napkins, curtain tie-backs or whatever you fancy. Take a look at the design of the second cushion as well if your ideas dry up. The photographs below show that it's as easy as one, two, three: stamp, paste, blow ...

You will need

white cotton fabric; scissors; guineafowl stamp; stamping pad; medium brush; fabric paint; round stickers; liquid fabric paint; atomiser; paper towels; polyester filling

1 Cut out the panels for the cushion. Apply a thin layer of fabric paint to the stamp: black to the body of the guineafowl, and burgundy to the head and feet. Dab the stamp onto the stamping pad and saturate the pad with paint according to the printed pattern.

2 Lightly dab the stamp into the paint, making sure that the paint adheres to the entire stamping surface without any paint collecting in the grooves. Carefully place the stamp in the right position on the cushion front panel and press down hard so that the paint is printed evenly. Lift the stamp and stamp again slightly higher over the one side without dabbing it in the paint again. In this way you will achieve a shadow effect that adds dimension. Repeat the stamping as desired and leave to dry.

3 Lay down adhesive tape 3 cm from the edge to frame the cushion and stick round stickers around the frame. Spray black liquid paint around the taped edge. Dab the stickers and adhesive tape with paper towels before peeling them off. Iron the decorated panel when the paint is dry to heat-set it.

4 Sew the cushion as described on page 99 and stuff with polyester filling.

126

FABRIC PAINT

Index

acetate 52, 105
acetone 11
adhesive lead 12
appliqué glue 84, 97
atomiser 67, 112, 114, 125
bathroom mat 65, 109, 110, 111
batik design 84
batik lampshade 77
bed lamp 89, 90, 91
bedding role 77, 80, 81
blind 47, 62, 65, 83, 84-87, 100, 101, 104, 105, 108, 109
   design for 87
   with ceiling drape 62, 106, 107
block method 23, 92, 97, 101
bookmark 52
brooch 32, 33
brushes 64
butterfly design 27
butterfly mobile 26, 27
candle ball 58, 59
candle holder 56, 57, 59, 123
canvas chair with decorated cushion 77, 78, 79
ceiling drape 62, 106, 107
ceramic clay 24, 38
chair cover 70, 71, 73
check pattern 121
Christmas decorations 43
clam design 115
clock mechanism 48
coasters 52, 53
colour spray 112, 125
containers, designs for 37
cooldrink can 17, 33
   cutting a 12
   strips 12
costume jewellery 32
crescent design 20
curling technique 10
curly jewellery 28
curly roses 28, 33
cushion cover 68, 126, 127
daisy design 98
decorated containers 36, 37
découpage 36
design 11
   enlargement of 23
   for earring 30
   for pendant 30
disco balls 42, 43

drape 106
earring design 30
earrings 31, 32, 33
Egyptian queen design 23
embossed pattern 34
embossing 17, 32, 34
enlarging designs 11
eraser stamp 66, 106, 108, 118, 122
fabric paint 63
   basic requirements 64
   basic techniques 64
   hints and tips 65
   liquid 64, 67 112
   thick 64
fabric protector 71, 72, 74
fabric stamp 66
fan blades 46, 47
fish design 115
fishy throw 114
fleur-de-lis candle holder 18, 22
fleur-de-lis design 122
floor mat 102
flower cushion cover 98, 99
flower design
   for fan blades 47
   for foiled frame 35
flower pot, decorated 101
flowing paint effect 52
foiled frame 34
frame 76
   cooldrink can 14
   for loose rug 74
   mirror 40, 41
   photo 40
   picture 34
freehand painting 64, 111
fridge magnet 16, 17
fruit design 101
geometric animal design 83
geometric designs 56
geometric patterns 83
giftwrap, designs from 51
glass lampshade 46
glass paint 9, 10, 13
   applying 11
   basic method 13
   basic requirements 11
glass painting, art of 9
glass table top 44, 54
glass top, decorated 44, 45, 54, 55

hubcap wall-clock 48, 49
imitation leather mats 102, 103
inflatable ball 43
jeans and shirt with fabric paint finish 118, 119
jewellery 30, 31, 32
kelim 82, 83
lampshade 50, 51, 76
lead outline 13
lead tape 12
leaf stamp 67
light fitting 45, 73
liquid fabric paint 64
liquid lead 11, 13
lizard design 45, 68
loose chair cover 94, 95
magazine holder 123
make-up tin 24, 25
mirror frame 40, 41
Modge Podge 36, 51
octopus design 36
outliner, fabric paint 64
paint, fixing of 65
papier-mâché 91
parchment 51
parrot design 17
pattern, repeating a 64
pendant 31
pendant design 30
perspex
   blades 46
   circle 44
   container 38, 39
perspex panel 23
   decorated 22, 60
picture frame 34
place-mat 72, 73, 102
plastic cooldrink bottle 10, 27, 28, 31, 56
plasticine stamp 114
playing card motifs 48, 97
polystyrene container 66,
polystyrene stamp 68, 88, 92
   make your own 68
potato stamp 108
pulley 86
   mechanism 85, 86
   system 87
recycling 9, 63
room divider 96, 97
rose design 28
round lamp cover 58

rug frame 74
scatter cushions 68, 69, 75, 127
screen 92, 93
seahorse design 36
self-adhesive plastic 10, 56
serviette 29, 124, 125
   holder 28
   ring 29
shadow printing 126
shortcut batik 67, 76, 84, 105, 106
sponging effect 11
spray effect 67
spray paint 67
   effect 112, 113, 114, 115
spraying technique 67
stained glass 9
stamp
   eraser 66
   plasticine 67
   potato 67
   string 67
stamping method 28, 29, 66, 76
stamping pad 66
   make your own 67
stamping technique 117
star design 20
starfish design 115
starch masking method 65, 101
stickers 18, 20, 21, 28, 29
string printing 79, 80
string stamp 120
sun design 20, 39
   for glass table top 54
sun stamp 120
tablecloth 29, 124, 125
tall lamp with perspex panels 60
tartan effect 98, 112
three-dimensional appliqué 99
tin frame 14, 15
tin strips 12, 13, 24
toilet mat 18
toilet set 23, 110, 111, 122, 123
transparency 31, 53
tray liner 52
T-shirt 116, 117
tulip design 124, 125
upholstery, decorated 71
waistcoats 120, 121
wall hanging headboard 88
watermelon design 102
window drape 18, 22, 108, 109

128